THE SCIENCE BEHIND THE FICTION

# BUILDING SCI-FI MOVIESCAPES

PROJECT MANAGER, ROTOVISION: LEONIE TAYLOR
COVER & INTERIOR DESIGN: ROTOVISION SA
ART DIRECTOR, ROTOVISION: LUKE HERRIOTT
ACQUISITION EDITOR, FOCAL PRESS: AMY JOLLYMORE
ASSISTANT EDITOR, FOCAL PRESS: CARA ANDERSON
MARKETING MANAGER, FOCAL PRESS:
CHRISTINE DEGON

FOCAL PRESS IS AN IMPRINT OF ELSEVIER
30 CORPORATE DRIVE, SUITE 400, BURLINGTON,
MA 01803, USA
LINACRE HOUSE, JORDAN HILL, OXFORD OX2 8DP, UK
WWW.FOCALPRESS.COM

ROTOVISION SA, SHERIDAN HOUSE,
112-116A WESTERN ROAD, HOVE,
EAST SUSSEX BN3 1DD, ENGLAND
TEL:+44 (0)1273 727 268 FAX:+44 (0)1273 727 269
E-MAIL: SALES@ROTOVISION.COM
WWW.ROTOVISION.COM

IMAGE

Ø1  *Star Wars* offered seminal future
architectural environments.

THE SCIENCE BEHIND THE FICTION

# BUILDING SCI-FI MOVIESCAPES

MATT HANSON

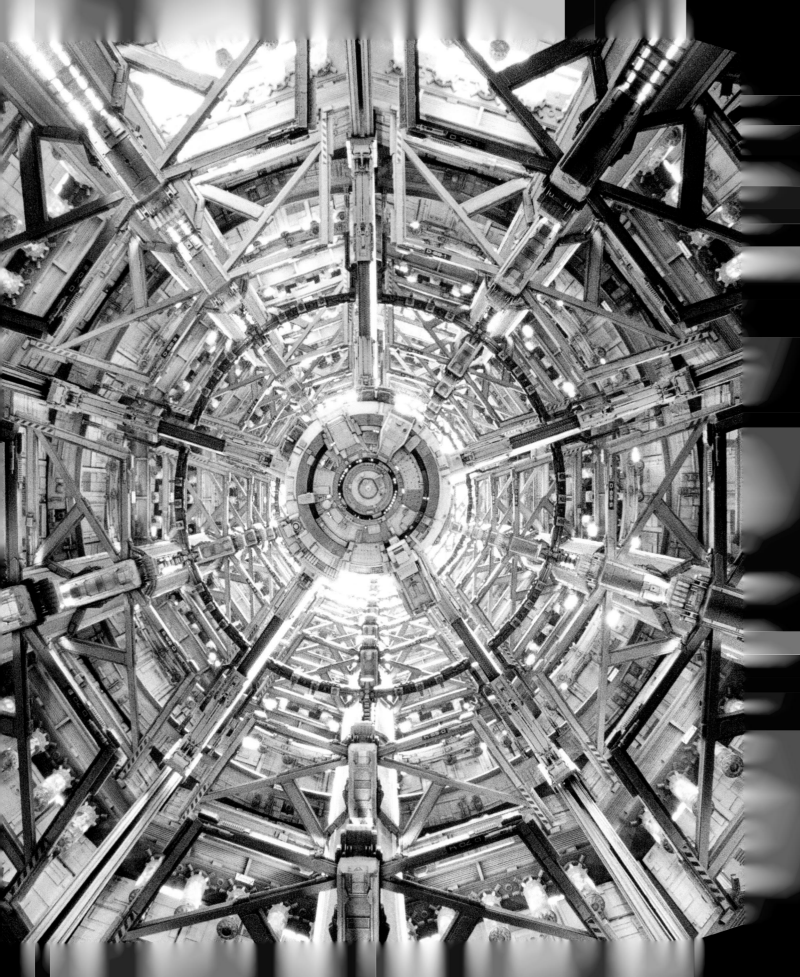

# FUTURE
# PERFECT
# IMPERFECT

## SCIENCE FICTION IS PEERLESS AS A FRAMING DEVICE FOR OUR CONCERNS. THE USE OF DIGITAL EFFECTS TO MAP AND TEXTURE THE VIRTUAL ENVIRONMENTS THAT CONSTRUCT THESE FICTIONS ONLY ENHANCES ITS EFFICACY.

If we look at movies of the past, the future appeared further away. In the twenty-first century, the future accelerates toward us at a dizzying pace—like Neo in *The Matrix* (see page 104), bending time-space and a virtual city in his wake. We are all living in the future in some way, and no doubt this is reflected in the increasing preeminence of science fiction cinema. Seeing into the future, gazing into that crystal ball, has always been a very human preoccupation, and we have never been as obsessed with it as we are now. Millennial pressures pull apart present day certainties and, as they do, we look to invent a future that we can somehow solve. Science fiction films act as a useful cultural barometer, touchstones for the hot-button topics of the day. In them, things can be said that are left unresolved and unspoken in the everyday.

The worlds created by science fiction cinema—whether full-blown fantasy or fiction a few degrees separated from the facts of the real world—have always been more about our present than the future they purport to predict. With the blossoming of digital effects, these visions have become increasingly bold, more seductive, visceral. The devices to recreate these fantasies, these simulacra, become ever more advanced. They have an amplified power to allure and revolt audiences, with glimpses into technologically fantastic worlds or dystopic societies that challenge our present status quo. >>>

IMAGE

LEFT & PREVIOUS PAGE
*Natural City* (see page 122).
A Korean vision of a dystopic
near-future citystate.

Ø1

Ø2

*Star Wars: A New Hope* (1977) was a landmark in effects-driven science fiction film (or science fantasy, as the purists would have it), just as Kubrick's *2001: A Space Odyssey* (1968) was in terms of bringing the genre onto the serious filmmaking agenda. But this book really begins in the early 1980s, because this was when the modern science fiction film was born. 1982 was the year that saw the seminal movies *Blade Runner* (see page 18) and *Tron* (see page 24) released. Both have cast their shadow over our cinematic visions of the future over since.

Vivian Sobchack labeled *Blade Runner*'s look as "future noir," a style that updates the urban dystopia, chaos, and sprawl that existed in that earliest and most influential sci-fi, *Metropolis* (1927). *Tron* has been analyzed less, but accurately foreshadowed the growing contemporary focus on virtually inflected worlds, with its groundbreaking use of computer graphics to create a digital arcade milieu.

This book is about those internal and external spaces, and the subsequent evolution of these environments. Science fiction is peerless as a framing device for our concerns. The use of digital effects to map and texture virtual environments that construct these fictions only enhances its efficacy.

We are in a golden age of building fantasies. The dream makers who construct cinematic images take their inspiration from myriad architectural influences—unsurprising, considering that architects are concerned with the invention and design of environments in which humanity can evolve and live in the decades ahead. In turn, our spaces are becoming progressively more cinematic as the future gets nearer and digital entertainment visions loop and feed back into architectural reality.

It is noteworthy that, as we become steeped in invisible networks of data and information, science fiction environments have become more involved with the augmented and virtual realities of digital space and how we as humans orient ourselves around this shifting relationship with our physical and non-physical habitats. Films like *i, Robot* (page 124), the *Animatrix* series, and *A.I. Artificial Intelligence* (page 78) delve back into the central paradox of our relationship with technology—techno-fear and techno-lust. As the environments and machines become more intelligent around us, do we as humans become more insignificant, less unique in the cosmos? Whether the individual film is about genetics, nanotechnology, the nuclear holocaust, race, class, power, or interplanetary war and terrorism, it all comes back to the question of what makes us sui generis. The best futurescapes are created to explore and reflect this fact.

IMAGES

Ø1  The design of *The Fifth Element* (see page 60) belies its French graphic art heritage.
Ø2  *A.I. Artificial Intelligence* (see page 78) production painting.
Ø3  *Star Wars* (see page 72): science fantasy colonization of Space.
Ø4  *Natural City* (see page 122): dawn of a new future?

# YESTERDAY'S TOMORROWS
## THE PRE-DIGITAL ERA

So it all began with *Le Voyage Dans La Lune* (1902) by Georges Méliès. A glimpse into an off-world, outer-space experience. A film which luxuriated in spectacle, in "voyages extraordinares." This has come to define the boundaries of the science fiction film genre, and find its apotheosis in today's genre giants. But it was another pioneer of cinema, Sergei Eisenstein, who, while essaying on some sketches of the Neoclassical engraver Giovanni Piranesi (a huge and continuing influence on movie set design), equated architectural composition itself to cinematic montage, and developed a theory of "space constructions." He argued that architecture is film's natural predecessor in transitioning between real and imaginary movement, bringing the spectator into new worlds, new spaces.

It is fitting, therefore, that the first real science fiction feature film, *Metropolis* (1927)—the template for innumerable successors—was created by the architecturally trained director, Fritz Lang. *Metropolis* replays the Frankenstein myth, with scientist Rotwang animating Maria, the first android in motion pictures. Workers are enslaved far underground to run the machines which keep Metropolis running smoothly, while the elite who run the city above live in luxury, cavorting in pleasure gardens and grandiose spaces. Lang was interested in exploring new environments, in generating visual impact through the creation of this cinematic space, and the film casts a stylistic influence simply because of this.

H.G. Wells, the renowned science fiction novelist and visionary, berated the film's view of the future city developing with vertical strata as outdated. But Lang's view, heavily influenced by his experience of New York City, has been remarkably prescient. It has cast its shadow over the decades, marking Manhattan as the most imagined and futuristic city non pareil. Only the emergence of Tokyo in the last decade can compete as the leading urban environment of the genre.

Lang's distorted cityscapes, his monumental New Tower of Babel—co-developed by Erich Kettelhut, Otto Hunte, and Lang himself—have been revisited and reworked through subsequent decades, but this application of the avant garde architectural thinking of the time was not isolated. Soviet sci-fi *Aelita: Queen of Mars* (1924), by Jakov Protazanov, featured Martian architecture modeled on idealist Russian revolutionary architecture. The film's design is built on the minimalist foundations of Le Corbusier's Plan Voisin of 1922, just as Lang's urban constructs mirror Antonio Sant'Elia's Citta Futurista. Protazanov's Mars is not dissimilar to the alien constructs of *Total Recall* (see page 40) over 50 years later.

Through the 1930s, and 1940s, science fiction concerned itself more with off-world pulp adventure and speculation. *The Shape of Things to Come* (1936, directed by William Cameron Menzies; an adaptation of the H.G. Wells' novel of the same name) surveys "Everytown" through 100 years, and draws influences from the work of Le Corbusier, the glass towers of Mies van der Rohe, and the more abstract designs of László Moholy-Nagy to negate the notion of high-rise urban canyons in the future.

>>>

IMAGES

01 *Metropolis*: Fritz Lang's film spawned a new vision of the future.
02 *Star Wars*: re-working of mythical themes in a galaxy far, far away.

It wasn't until Jean-Luc Godard's *Alphaville* (1965), that a radically different template of science fiction environments was established. Together with cinematographer Raoul Coutard, Godard shot Paris as if it was an alien environment. The minimalist mise-en-scène—neutral and bleak—was also apparent in Francois Truffaut's *Fahrenheit 451* (1966). These films in turn foreshadow our contemporary "future documentaries."

Stanley Kubrick's seminal *2001: A Space Odyssey* (1968) took science fiction to a new level, transcending its pulp, speculative roots to become a serious narrative playground to explore the philosophical and sociological. Science fiction became more scientific, technological, and immediate, as the moon landing in 1969 brought Space into our homes. *Solaris* (1972) by Andrei Tarkovsky turned Kubrick's outer-space abstractions toward inner space. The claustrophobia of these early space environments provided the perfect setting for exploring the human psyche.

Science fiction began to sing to a new tune with the the space opera of *Star Wars* (1977). With it, George Lucas invented the modern special effects blockbuster, and fueled the imagination of countless cinemagoers. He brought to the genre the unlimited possibilities of what could be visualized on screen. In so doing, he seeded science fiction's increasing popularity and sealed its future course.

Cinema's indulgence in the sensual immediacy of the viewing experience, of on-screen display, is nothing new (as we know from Lang's original declaration), but it has been taken to new heights with digital effects and computer-generated imagery. Modern society's scopophilic tendency—our love of looking—is generously fulfilled by the thrilling spectacle and futurespaces documented in this book. A cinema of spectacle rewarding our attentions as much as narrative. Science fiction film's time has come.

**IMAGES**

**01** *THX 1138 (1971)*: science fiction often voices our concerns about future technology and artificial intelligence.
**02** *2001: A Space Odyssey* (left, & over page): Space becomes the playground for our future fears and fantasies.

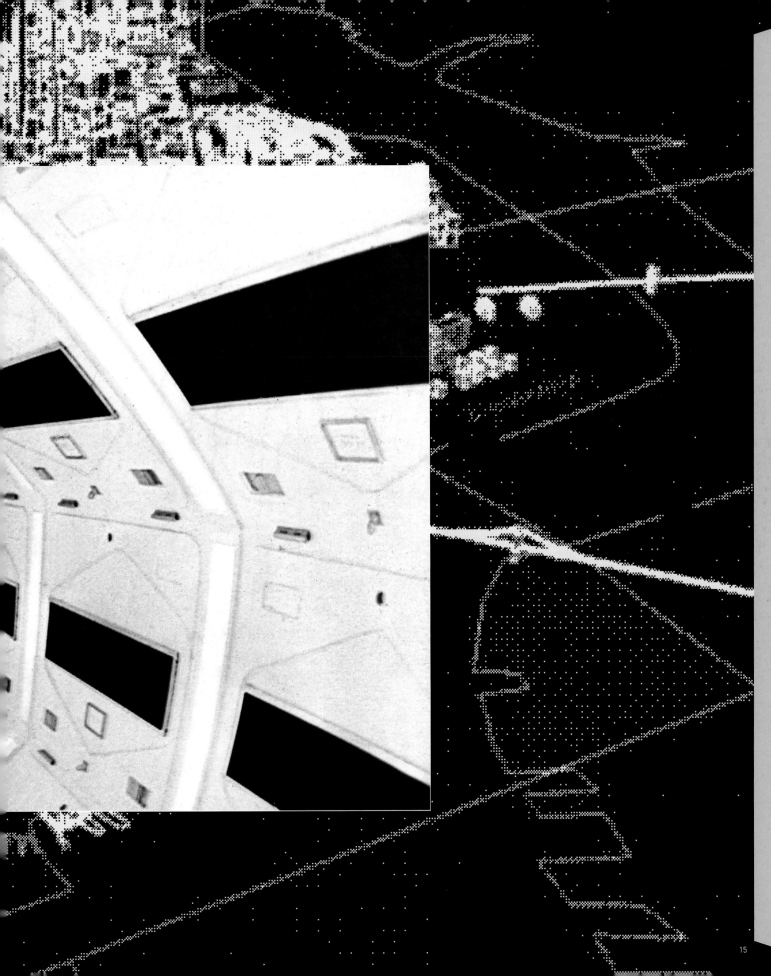

# THE FILMS
# DIGITAL-ERA
# SCIENCE FICTION
# 1982-2004

**CREDITS**
DIRECTOR: RIDLEY SCOTT
PRODUCTION DESIGNER: LAWRENCE G. PAULL
VISUAL FUTURIST: SYD MEAD
SCREENPLAY: HAMPTON FANCHER, DAVID PEOPLES
BASED ON THE NOVEL: "DO ANDROIDS DREAM OF ELECTRIC SHEEP?" BY PHILIP K. DICK
PRODUCER: MICHAEL DEELEY

2004
2003
2002
2001
2000
1999
1998
1997
1996
1995
1994
1993
1992
1991
1990
1989
1988
1987
1986
1985
1984
1983

# BLADE RUNNER

+ ENTERTAINMENT EFFECTS GROUP (EEG), DREAM QUEST IMAGES (DQI), ANATOMORPHEX

**1982**  FILM

VISUAL EFFECTS

02

Over a quarter of a century since it was first produced, this epochal future noir classic is still a benchmark in creating an atmospheric, captivating milieu of the future. Ridley Scott's talent at generating outstanding mise-en-scène assured *Blade Runner* its landmark status in the genre. Famously Scott wanted a "film set forty years hence, made in the style of forty years ago."[1] The style created by the execution of these instructions, the perfect mood and environments, has cast a long shadow over the genre ever since.

Scott's original conception of the setting of *Blade Runner* was as a vast megalopolis comprising two cities—one of them being New York—that had grown together (in the vein of Tokyo-Osaka). After discarding the options for shooting on location, the primary set became the "Old New York City Street" at the Warner Bros Lot (at the time called the Burbank Studios), which had been used in classic film noir's such as *The Maltese Falcon* (1941) and *The Big Sleep* (1946). Production designer Lawrence G. Paull, along with Syd Mead, the film's Visual Futurist, retrofitted this set, layering it with pipes, tubing, neon signs—the flotsam and jetsam of the future—to fast-forward it into the world of 2019. The set meshed western architectural elements from Manhattan avenues and London's Piccadilly Circus, with Asian-influenced street life from Tokyo's Omotesando, and Hong Kong's bustling Wanchai district.

>>>

"I BROUGHT IN JUST ABOUT MY ENTIRE ARCHITECTURAL RESEARCH LIBRARY... WE TURNED THE PHOTOGRAPHS SIDEWAYS, UPSIDE DOWN, INSIDE OUT, AND BACKWARDS TO STRETCH WHERE WE WERE GOING AND CAME UP WITH A STREET THAT LOOKED LIKE **CONAN THE BARBARIAN** IN 2020." LAWRENCE G. PAULL

2004
2003
2002
2001
2000
1999
1998
1997
1996
1995
1994
1993
1992
1991
1990
1989
1988
1987
1986
1985
1984
1983
**1982**

Ø1

While Scott's masterly eye for art direction sets him firmly as the ultimate designer of the picture, it fell to Paull to make the variety of sets come to life. "For all the buildings we did, I brought in all the photographs from Milan, and we took photographs of arcades, columns, classical things, and all the architecture," explains Paull. "I brought in just about my entire architectural research library, and we went from Egyptian to Deco to Streamline Moderne to Classical, from Frank Lloyd Wright to Antonio Gaudí. We turned the photographs sideways, upside down, inside out, and backwards to stretch where we were going and came up with a street that looked like *Conan the Barbarian* in 2020. That's basically where we were headed, because it had to be richly carved. I didn't want right angles; I didn't want slick surfaces."[2]

The film mixes some of L.A.'s real-life locations with backlot sets, from using Union Station to create the art-deco-tinged Police Headquarters, to Sebastian's home in the Bradbury building, and Frank Lloyd Wright's Ennis Brown House which inspired and was used for filming Deckard's apartment. Other memorable locations made from sets and miniatures include Little Tokyo, Animoid Row, and the Tyrell Corporation pyramidal headquarters.

*Blade Runner's* stunning vistas are evident from the film's opening: the hazy, nightmare vision of the Hades Landscape—L.A.'s industrialized, never-ending suburbs—is the defining shot of modern sci-fi. Paul M. Sammon, writer of the definitive book on the film, *Future Noir: The Making of Blade Runner*, describes it well: "This hellish environment is dotted by dozens of fireball-belching cracking towers cocooned in a thick petrochemical haze. Strange futuristic vehicles zip by in the polluted sky overhead."[3]

>>>

IMAGES

Ø1 The Hades cityscape emphasized the industrial sprawl surrounding future L.A.
Ø2 The huge televisual billboards became a signature of the *Blade Runner* environment.
Ø3 Megastructures were suffused in an authentic L.A. smog.

"BLADE RUNNER BYPASSED THE USUAL, SIMPLISTIC CONDEMNATION OF URBAN SPRAWL BY EMPHASIZING THE UNEXPECTED BEAUTY LURKING WITHIN INDUSTRIAL ROT."
PAUL M. SAMMON

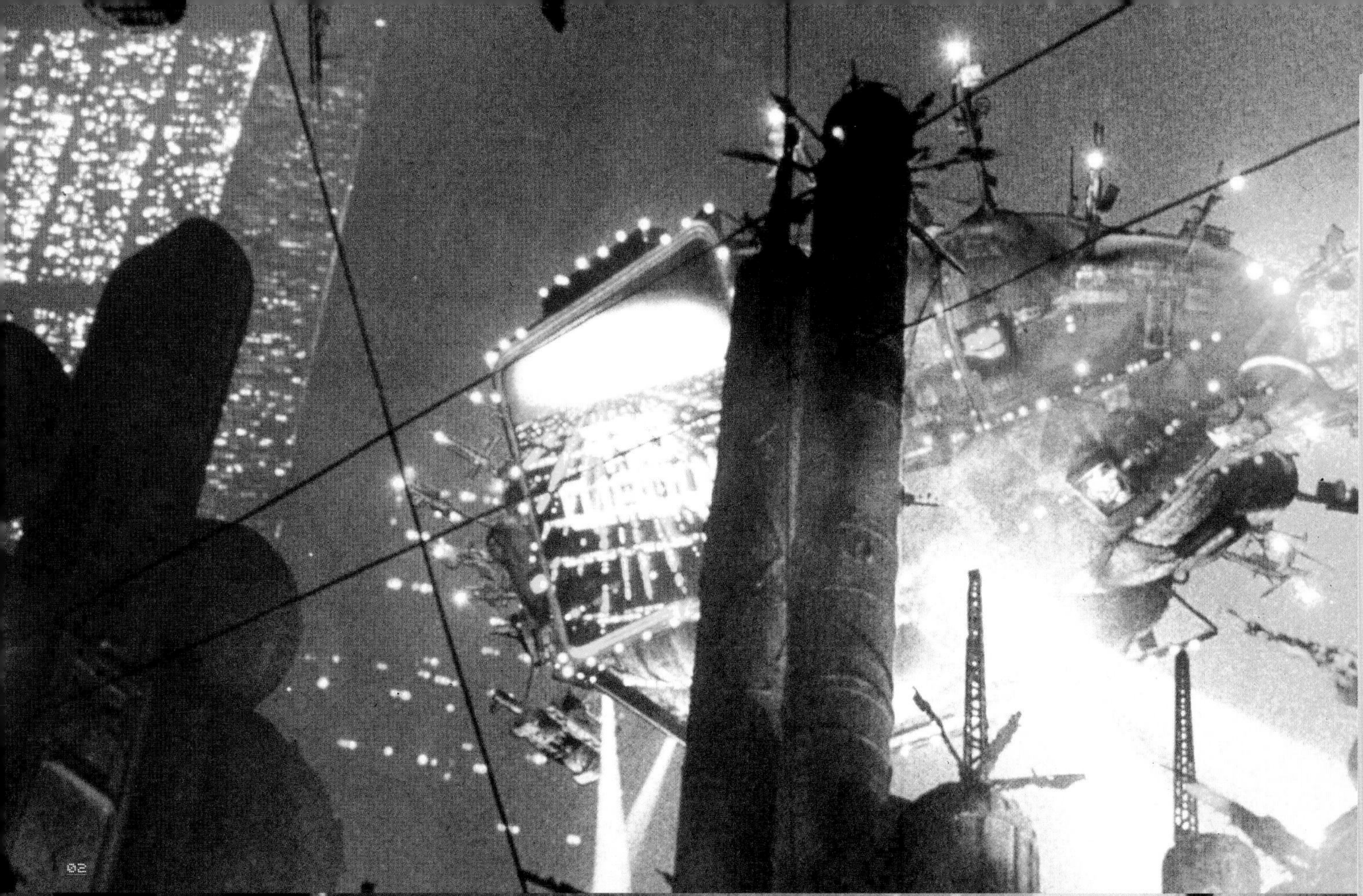

02

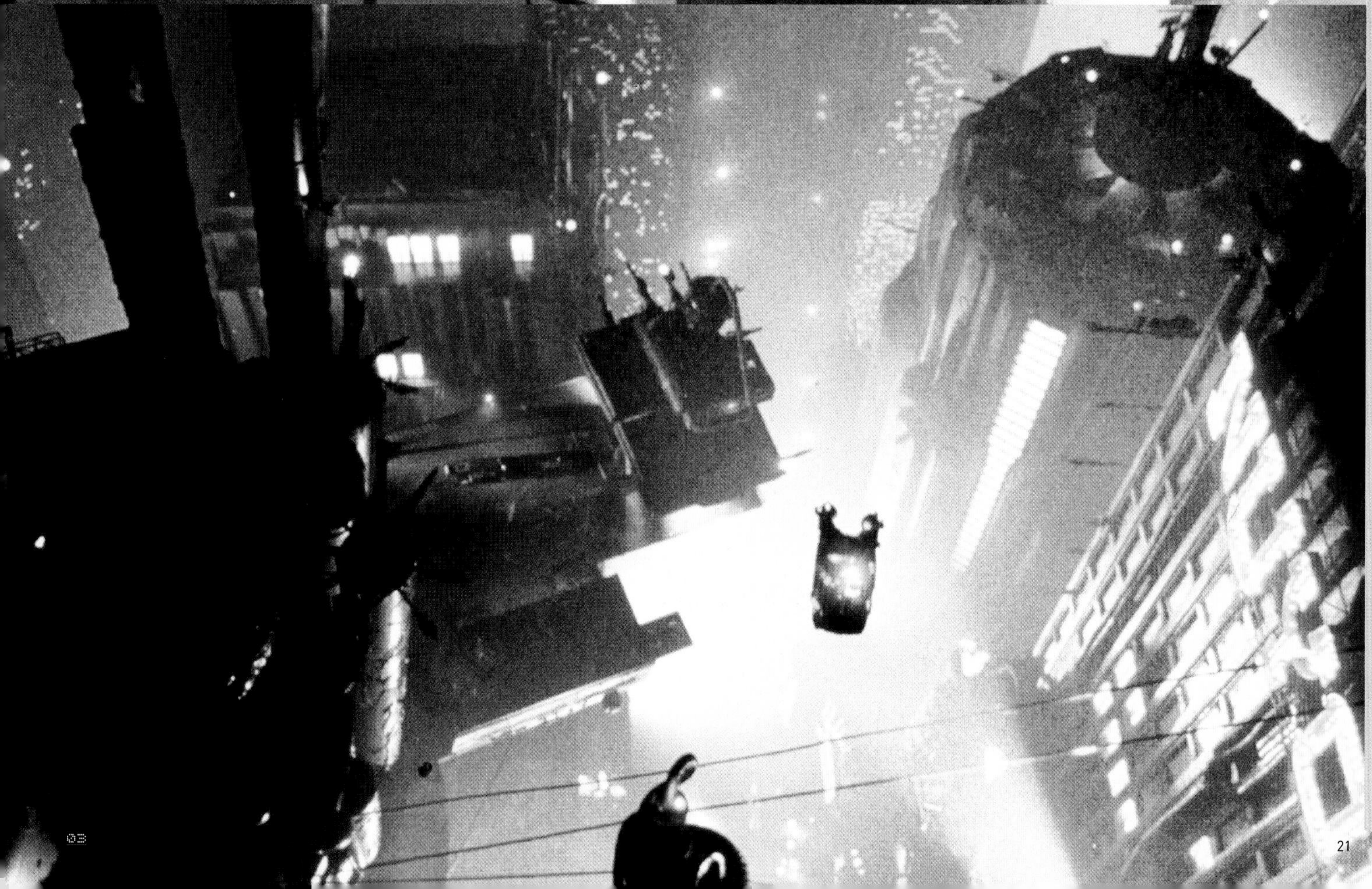

03

01

2004
2003
2002
2001
2000
1999
1998
1997
1996
1995
1994
1993
1992
1991
1990
1989
1988
1987
1986
1985
1984
1983
**1982**

02

03

"*Blade Runner*'s creators made a canny choice when they elected to set its story only 37 years after 1982, the year *Blade Runner* was released,"[4] notes Sammon. "By placing his film a mere four decades ahead of the time he was making it, Ridley Scott was able to more realistically depict what Los Angeles might theoretically be like in 2019. So, in that respect *Blade Runner*—which takes great pains to logically extend the appearance and functionality of 1980s-style buildings, vehicles, fashions, and machines, into early-twenty-first-century manifestations of those same objects—can be said to have successfully portrayed a believable near future. Even if it is a decaying, callous, dystopic one."

Influential architectural concepts such as Peter Cook's Trickling Towers of 1978— a proposition of megastructures that were actively altered and redefined through their lifespan by inhabitants (retrofitted)—all add to a sense of a convincing alternate future. But a certain dissonance is still evident. Sammon continues, "*Blade Runner*'s 2019 L.A. may appear believable, but the real Los Angeles is a city whose architecture is defined by horizontal sprawl and an endless carpet of suburban subdivisions, not by the relatively tiny percentage of closely-packed skyscrapers that currently dominate L.A.'s downtown skyline. This means that *Blade Runner*'s mostly vertical buildings actually look like they belong on a twenty-first-century Manhattan, not in 2019 L.A."

The reason for this confusion? Preproduction flip-flopped the location between the fictional megacity of San Angeles, spreading from San Francisco down the US West Coast to Los Angeles, New York, and back to L.A. This fusion of the two great American cities, in a melting pot of architectural styles—the Mayan-inspired pyramids and 200-storey high-rise tower—is only now being superseded by digital effects to envision bizarre futuristic environments.

**[ SOURCES ]**

**[1]** "RETROFITTING THE FUTURE," JOANNE OSTROW, *Washington Post* (27/10/1981)

**[2]** *Lawrence G Paull, By Design: Interviews with Film Production Designers,* VINCENT LOBRUTTO, [WESTPORT: PRAEGER, 1992]

**[3]** *Future Noir: The Making of Blade Runner,* PAUL SAMMON, [ORION, 1997]

**[3]** PAUL M. SAMMON, ORIGINAL INTERVIEW, MATT HANSON [10/2004]

IMAGES

01 *Blade Runner* made full use of location to create some of the most memorable imagery in the genre.
02 The film's Asian influences are everywhere, from clothing to graffiti.
03 The neon environments of *Blade Runner* have been so emulated they are almost a cliché of the genre.

**CREDITS**
DIRECTOR: STEVEN LISBERGER
PRODUCTION DESIGNERS: JEAN GIRAUD, SYD MEAD, DEAN EDWARD MITZNER
SCREENPLAY: STEVEN LISBERGER, BONNIE MACBIRD
VISUAL EFFECTS SUPERVISORS: HARRISON ELLENSHAW, RICHARD TAYLOR
PRODUCER: DONALD KUSHNER

*Tron* is a visionary film that ushered in a new era of science fiction, the "virtual reality" sub-genre, replete with ground-breaking animated effects the like of which had never been seen before. With the world still in the era of the mainframe, on the brink of the home PC revolution, Director Steven Lisberger and his production team created the first feature film based around and featuring virtual sets and computer-generated environments.

*Tron* used approximately 1,200 laboriously produced special effects shots involving from 12 to 45 painstakingly composited layered elements to fuse live action with backlit, "glowing" animation effects and computer-generated landscapes. The production used up to 450 artists for this intensive effects work. They were creating a new type of animation—computer-generated imagery as a term hadn't even been coined at the time—where specific shots were often first-time attempts at creating effects nobody had ever done before.

# TRON

FILM

+ **ROBERT ABEL & ASSOCIATES, DIGITAL EFFECTS, INFORMATION INTERNATIONAL INC (TRIPLE-I), MATHEMATICAL APPLICATIONS GROUP (MAGI)**

**VISUAL EFFECTS**

02

03

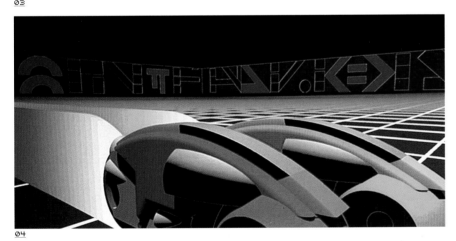

04

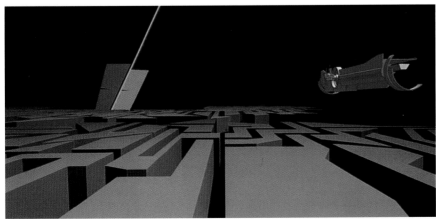

05

Before geeks were cool, this film was a geek's dream. The film's scenario called for a real world and a virtual one, described at the time as the "electronic world." The hero, video game hotshot Flynn is unjustly terminated from computer conglomerate ENCOM. The Master Control Program (MCP) is the virtual villain that has stolen some arcade game code from ENCOM's systems, initiated by the firm's head, Dillinger. Flynn hacks into his former employer's systems to clear his name and find the culprit. In trying to do this, he becomes digitized by a particle beam, and is turned into a data-stream. Transported into the virtual world of the mainframe—Lisberger's script anthropomorphosized the programs, routines, and electronic processes of the computer circuitry and internal code—he finds himself in an oppressive environment in which he is wanted for deletion.

The "electronic world" of *Tron*, a precursor to the array of cyberspace visions in the genre's future, is a literal and groundbreaking visualization. Fifteen minutes of bleeding-edge computer animation was at the core of the motion picture's narrative, with an additional 53 minutes of backlit animation involving live actors and sets. A computer-generated movie in an era when Macs and PCs were yet to be invented, the production used custom computer equipment "hot rods"—improvised early computing components—in a period where the vernacular of digital animation had yet to be rendered.

>>>

IMAGES

01–04 *Tron*'s synthesis with games worlds was truly ahead of its time. The gladiatorial challenges were reflected in *Tron*'s complementary arcade game produced by Bally.
02 Syd Mead designed the sharp lines of the tanks and Recognizers, both inside and out, that patrol the Mainframe.
03 Backlit animation complemented the minimal use of cutting-edge CGI in the film.
05 Lisberger's use of grids reminds him of the aerial view of L.A. on take off from L.A.X.

2004
2003
2002
2001
2000
1999
1998
1997
1996
1995
1994
1993
1992
1991
1990
1989
1988
1987
1986
1985
1984
1983
**1982**

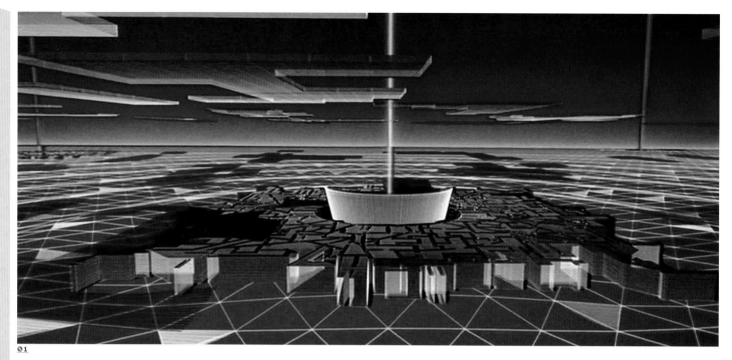

01

02

03

Lisberger's motivation for developing the project? "*Star Wars* started all this, with the Imperial mother ship going overhead. Your sensory receptors, your optical capabilities, were overwhelmed. It's something that Industrial Light & Magic has understood for a long time—how to overwhelm." [1]

While the CGI now looks crude and simplistic, the style is instantly recognizable as one all of *Tron's* own. The clean vector lines and flat shaded, often simply wireframe structures hold a nostalgia and authenticity to those of us brought up during the birth of the computer and videogame era, that transcends the technical limitations of the time. Like the world of painting before true perspective, *Tron's* animation is one before raytracing, and physics models. It features CG as fine art—handworked digital processes and analog techniques used to complement the production design. "The key was the backlight and compositing," noted Visual Effects Supervisor Harrison Ellenshaw. "The key was making live-action look like it was processed in the computer." [2]

Out of necessity, the production design evolved a simplified reality. The acid-etched nature of computer circuitry found its parallel in the electronic world sets. To achieve the unique look on set, actors performed on black stages, wearing white suits with black trim. Initially photographed on black and white film, the negative was then used as a source for 16x20-inch transparencies. Mattes could be made from these, and additional cel copies generated to be hand painted. The glowing lines that define the sets, the neon blue that dominates the film, along with magma reds, and acid greens and yellows, were used as color keys to convey emotion. Optical filters were utilized to affect and enhance the light. Methods included ripple glass effects, silkscreen steel mesh, exposure changes and hand-drawn frame manipulation.

Lisberger was particularly pleased with the relationship generated between these bleeding-edge digital techniques and analog animation methods: "I really was proud that we did all the backlight work that we did in Tron. There is a certain soulful quality to good old analog backlighting. In some ways, we've gone backwards—there's a sterility factor to some of these effects that are fully digital. You're in a funny place when one is constantly trying to take perfect digital effects and degrade them so they have this analog familiarity."

04

05

Triple-I and MAGI were the main suppliers of computer work in the movie. The companies built custom code and new systems to generate effects. Synthavision was a MAGI-built system that created simple 3D objects, such as cubes, cones, or spheres, and added to or subtracted these elements from each other to create different combinations of shapes. The system used true vector graphics, unlike modern computers which emulate this. The dataspace used vector graphic effects. The "3-space" movement through binary bitpatterns and the polygonal landscape was achieved through multiple camera passes. A traditional animation camera was pointed at a high resolution vector graphic computer screen, and frame by frame, using different color filters, the image was built up.

Lisberger's achievement in creating an artful electronic world has been underestimated. He was careful to surround himself with influential world-renowned artists to hone his vision of *Tron*. "It was a coup to have the juxtaposition of Syd Mead's powerful technical work in opposition to Moebius's soulful, lyrical design work." [3] Mead—from an industrial design background—and Moebius—from comic art—added an extra dimension to the production designs. Peter Lloyd completed the conceptual look of the neon and electronic elements.

*Tron* offers up minimalist but memorable moments in its virtual landscape: fractal mountains, wireframe canyons, deserts of data pulses, Sark's Carrier, the I/O Tower, and, at the mainframe's core, the Master Control Program structure. All rendered with originality and verve, ready to fill in with imagination.

[ SOURCES ]

[1] "TRON REVISITED," STEPHANIE ARGY *VFX Pro* (10/2000)

[2] IBID

[3] *Tron Special Edition* COMMENTARY (10/2004)

IMAGES

01 The team brought together by Disney to make *Tron*, and then discarded, would fragment and go on to revolutionize the animation and digital effects industry.
02–03 Mead's hard-edged vehicle designs perfectly complemented the vector visuals of *Tron*.
04 Beautiful angular architecture represented blocks of code.
05 Actors were painstakingly composited within environments using hand-created elements.

"THE KEY WAS THE BACKLIGHT AND COMPOSITING... MAKING LIVE-ACTION LOOK LIKE IT WAS PROCESSED IN THE COMPUTER."

HARRISON ELLENSHAW

2004
2003
2002
2001
2000
1999
1998
1997
1996
1995
1994
1993
1992
1991
1990
1989
1988
1987
1986
1985
1984
1983
1982

**CREDITS**

DIRECTOR: **DAVID LYNCH**
PRODUCTION DESIGNER: **ANTHONY MASTERS**
SCREENPLAY: **DAVID LYNCH**
BASED ON THE NOVEL: **FRANK HERBERT**
PRODUCER: **RAFFAELLA DE LAURENTIIS**

# DUNE

**FILM**

01

02

*Dune* stands out as a baroque sci-fi film, a world ripe in visual imagery not of the near-future extrapolations of many science-fiction movies, but of full-blown future fantasy, based on Frank Herbert's *Dune* saga. The diverse array of sci-fi worlds conjured up in David Lynch's adaptation of the novel resulted in meticulously produced interpretations of Arrakis, Geidi Prime, Caladan, and Kaitain—the home planets of the Great Houses of the Landsraad, featuring the Atreides, Harkonnen, and Emperor. The various factions are locked in a battle to control the spice drug Melange, which is used by the Space Guild's Navigators to "fold space."

Lynch's initial ambivalence to the subject matter freed him up to produce a left-field interpretation of *Dune*'s parallel worlds, where others had ground to a halt under the weight of expectations engendered by Herbert's wildly popular epic. Alexandro Jodorowsky and Ridley Scott's developments both stalled.

"I was never a science-fiction fan," Lynch reasoned after filming. "But Herbert's book incorporates dream sequences, complex textures, different levels of meaning, and symbolism; it concerns people, their emotions, their fears and goals—and also provides an opportunity to create whole new worlds by combining elements in ways that have never been done before... That works out fine because my movies are film-paintings—moving portraits captured on celluloid."[1]

Production designer Anthony Masters, a veteran of genre-defining films, having designed Kubrick's *2001: A Space Odyssey* (1968), was in charge of building over 70 sets. He quickly found Lynch worked best at refining the look of the material, editing suggestions that were inputted to him. Masters' guide from the Director in producing designs was simple: it mustn't look like other science-fiction films. Masters explains: "David didn't want the film to have a futuristic look; instead, we went to the past, to a 1950s style of over-elaborated, functionless decoration."[2]

>>>

IMAGES

01 The production had over 70 sets built. The Emperor's Palace and throne room had 24,000 gem-encrusted, styrofoam stalactite forms individually hung for decoration.
02 Original production painting of the Emperor's Palace by Ron Miller.

2004
2003
2002
2001
2000
1999
1998
1997
1996
1995
1994
1993
1992
1991
1990
1989
1988
1987
1986
1985
**1984**
1983
1982

"Caladan, the water planet, supports large forests, so the entire Atreides castle was built from hard wood carved into strange patterns. Its society, based on traditional military organization, utilizes many weapons made of wood and metal—especially gold. Arrakis, by contrast, is a dry planet, so we designed all sorts of paraphernalia for desert survival. My personal favorite, Geidi Prime, is an oil planet with one city; we used steel, bolts, and porcelain for construction. The Emperor's homeworld is sophisticated—and layered with gold. Herbert described many of the settings in the book, but we still had lots of leeway. We developed a concept for each planet, and every structure conformed to them."[3]

Finding inspiration in historical detail, each world developed from different national periods, with Venetian, Egyptian, and Victorian themes emerging. Masters used Ron Miller to derive production paintings. "I had a great deal of freedom and this was encouraged by both Tony and David," states Miller. "The general process—at least at the start—was for me to take Tony's sketches and from them invent what a scene in the film would look like. Since few of Tony's drawings were interpretations of specific scenes, I usually had to combine the contents of several different sketches—props, settings, et cetera—into what I thought looked reasonable and dramatic. Tony's sketches were always in B&W, so I had to come up with the color schemes and lighting. I rarely, if ever, followed any of Tony's drawings slavishly, but included a good deal of my own ideas and inventions."[4]

Miller went on to design all of the matte art for Al Whitlock to implement, many props for the film, and all of the various symbols and alphabets of the production.

Another element crucial in *Dune*'s look was the model building. Hanging and foreground miniatures were utilized extensively to produce the film's visual effects, along with matte backgrounds and process shots. Eric Swenson worked extensively on the miniatures crew: "On the main production in Mexico we did five months of what I would call 'hard' miniatures work which was all storyboarded. Brian Smithies directed the model unit. We dealt with crucial things such as the inside of the Navigator's highliner craft. This was all done by having several different scale models made—starting with the full craft at eight inches high and eight-foot long shot against a blue screen, then a 10-foot high by 20-foot wide section, and so on."[5]

Eight further months of miniatures and models shooting with a crew of four in Burbank followed, as Lynch compiled the footage and started the editing process. Swenson continues: "While working on the film, I remember it came across as very rich. The amount of detail on the sets was unprecedented in my opinion. I was 23 at the time, but having worked on many films since, I think that's still true.

"The fact the show was all going on in Mexico allowed the production to tap into a lot of cheap labor. There was, like, 20 guys working on a 6x6 foot area of carving—really detailed set work—and degrading it. The fretwork in the Emperor's Palace was astonishing.

"The diverse nature of the looks created was really helped by the international nature of the production. They were Italians, Americans, British, Spaniards... David was expert at welding all these visions together. Each film has its own culture. These different cultures create different animals. And the elements at play in *Dune* resulted in such a rich look."

Swenson created a special way to distort different fields and shapes as part of *Dune*'s unique block combat shield, along with extensive dream sequence footage for Lynch. "He had very specific ideas of the shots he wanted. Drops of water, a waving flag, eyeballs. We used a little 40x40 stage to set-up all these shots... This was all pre-digital, those effects wouldn't really come in until about five years later. At the time, everything was done using an optical printer."

*Dune* is a flawed masterwork. Its genius, like all of Lynch's work, lies in the quirks and impressions of production design, of the details and not the whole; in being able, in a pre-digital era, to encapsulate and envision *Dune*'s worlds.

[ SOURCES ]

[1] "DUNE, FILM PREVIEW," BRENDAN STRASSER, *Prevue 58* (1984)

[2] "MASTER BUILDERS OF DUNE," PATRICIA RIDDLE, *Film Preview 56* (1984)

[3] AS [1].

[4] RON MILLER, ORIGINAL INTERVIEW, MATT HANSON, (10/2004)

[5] ERIC SWENSON, ORIGINAL INTERVIEW, MATT HANSON, (11/2004)

"DAVID LYNCH DIDN'T WANT THE FILM TO HAVE A FUTURISTIC LOOK; INSTEAD, WE WENT TO THE PAST, TO A 1950S STYLE OF OVER-ELABORATED, FUNCTIONLESS DECORATION." TONY MASTERS

IMAGES

01 The organic world of Caladan. House Atreides uses predominantly wooden, natural material.
02 In contrast, the Harkonnen's homeworld of Geidi Prime uses "artificial" colors and industrial hues.

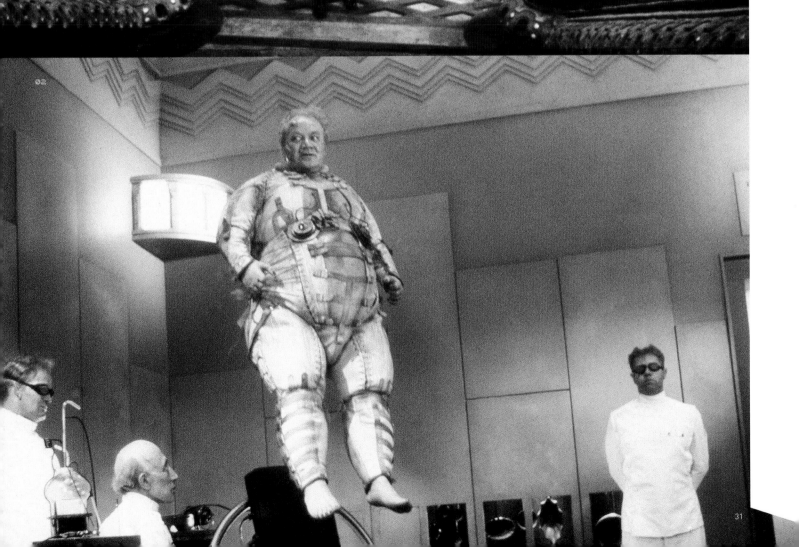

01

02

2004
2003
2002
2001
2000
1999
1998
1997
1996
1995
1994
1993
1992
1991
1990
1989
1988
1987
1986
**1985**
1984
1983
1982

01

04

02

05

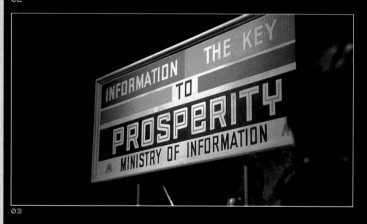

03

06

# BRAZIL

**FILM**

**CREDITS**

DIRECTOR: **TERRY GILLIAM**
PRODUCTION DESIGNER: **NORMAN GARWOOD**
ART DIRECTORS: **JOHN BEARD, KEITH PAIN**
WRITTEN BY: **TERRY GILLIAM, TOM STOPPARD, CHARLES MCKEOWN**
PRODUCER: **ARNON MILCHAN**

07

08

09

*Brazil* is a satirical vision à la *1984* from arch-fantastist Terry Gilliam. In it he creates a world that looks like, as he describes in the book, *Gilliam on Gilliam* [1]: "Everywhere in the twentieth century, on the Los Angeles/Belfast border." The film has a good case for being the ne plus ultra of fantasy urban dystopias. The spaces of *Brazil* are a masterful blend of the surreal and all-too-real. Corporate architecture, and the ever-expanding metropolis—spouting cables, pipes, and ducts—are parodied and reimagined as an inescapable nightmare.

Gilliam describes the evolution of these spaces: "It was so clear when we were writing it that there were two parallel worlds—the real world and the dream world—and the story in the dream world was a complete tale in itself... What had happened was the real world was proving so bizarre that there was no need for the dreams. For example, when I pulled out all the guts of [Sam's] flat, they were hanging like entrails; but there was a dream sequence where Sam tries to cut through a forest of these entrails with his mighty sword. But there was no need for the dream once we'd done it in Sam's 'real' world."

Sam Lowry (played by Jonathan Pryce) is an administrative error in a retro-future, lost in a bureaucratic world of whimsy. His adventures take in locations that veer from his drearily municipal (and malfunctioning) flat to a nightmarish cooling tower reappropriated as a operatic scaled torture chamber. *Brazil*'s "cyborg architecture"[2] is used to contain and confuse the human spirit, insinuating itself into the soul of city dwellers, the better to contain them.
>>>

IMAGES

01–06 *Brazil*'s idea of industrialism, totalitarianism, and absurdism, gone wild are perfectly illustrated by set design, and miniatures.
07–09 One party, one architecture. Larger than life, fascistically designed environments emphasize the belittling of the individual in *Brazil*'s world.

2004
2003
2002
2001
2000
1999
1998
1997
1996
1995
1994
1993
1992
1991
1990
1989
1988
1987
1986
**1985**
1984
1983
1982

Ø1

"GET ME DR. ELIOT—IT'S URGENT"

**CANNON ELECTRIC**

Ø2

JULY 1957                    35 CENTS

**POPULAR MECHANICS**
MAGAZINE
WRITTEN SO YOU CAN UNDERSTAND IT

HILLER'S AERIAL SEDAN
—your flying car for 1967—page 74
Stand by for Satellite Take-Off!
Owners Report: OLDSMOBILE
HOW TO OUTSMART HOUSEBREAKERS

Ø3

Gilliam has expressed his love of London's diverse building styles, and he took advantage of these to stretch his budget to the scope of his imagination. In the film, Croydon Power Station doubles up as the film's Ministry, while variously the National Liberal Club, Lord Leighton's house, and Victoria Dock's warehouses and grain silos, were all used as exteriors or as the basis of sets. These locations were all dressed in a retro-futurist style.

The Director's vision owes as much to the utopian vision of America in the 1940s as it does to Orwell's *1984*. Posters helped extend this world and create a world out of sight of the camera, advertising holidays and consumer goods. John Beard, the film's Art Director, pillaged his magazine collection for old issues of *Science and Mechanics* and suchlike; "Terry Gilliam wanted the film to look retro-futuristic, and I had a lot of comics and magazines from the 1930s, which we used as reference material for the vehicles in the film. The ideas they illustrated were bold, pure, and clean."[3] The research process was about creating a "melting pot" of ideas and influences from which to expand on this retro-futuristic kernel.

"For me, architecture in the film is as much a set of characters as those that speak and wear clothes," says Gilliam. "All the sets have a function within the whole process, they represent specific ideas."[1]

The key influences of *Brazil*'s architecture lies in the work of Hugh Ferriss, the American illustrator of architectural futures (giving rise to the oversized, corporate mega-structures), and the Pompidou Centre in Paris (the duct-ridden living spaces of the workers). *Brazil*'s world is so successful because it creates such an exotic fantasy made up from feasible (and often mundane) architectural reality.

"FOR ME, ARCHITECTURE IN THE FILM IS AS MUCH A SET OF CHARACTERS AS THOSE THAT SPEAK AND WEAR CLOTHES. ALL THE SETS HAVE A FUNCTION WITHIN THE WHOLE PROCESS, THEY REPRESENT SPECIFIC IDEAS."
*TERRY GILLIAM*

FEBRUARY 1951        35 CENTS

# POPULAR MECHANICS
## MAGAZINE
WRITTEN SO YOU CAN UNDERSTAND IT

*See page 118*

04

【 SOURCES 】

[1] *Gilliam on Gilliam*, ED. IAN CHRISTIE, (FABER & FABER, 1999)

[2] *Architecture & Film: Vol 2*, ED. BOB FEAR, ARCHITECTURAL DESIGN SERIES (2000)

[3] *Production Design & Art Direction* (SCREENCRAFT), PETER ETTEDGUI, (ROTOVISION, 1999)

IMAGES

01–04 The peculiar esthetic of *Brazil* stems from the total immersion in period industrial design, gleaned from the Art Director's collection of 1930s magazines, setting it apart in appearance and giving rise to a striking visual legacy.

2004
2003
2002
2001
2000
1999
1998
1997
1996
1995
1994
1993
1992
1991
1990
1989
1988
1987
1986
1985
1984
1983
1982

01

# BATMAN

**FILM**

**CREDITS**

DIRECTOR: **TIM BURTON**

PRODUCTION DESIGNER: **ANTON FURST**

ART DIRECTION: **TERRY ACKLAND-SNOW, NIGEL PHELPS**

SCREENPLAY: **SAM HAMM, WARREN SKAAREN**

STORY: **SAM HAMM**

PRODUCERS: **PETER GUBER, JON PETERS**

VISUAL EFFECTS SUPERVISOR: **DEREK MEDDINGS**

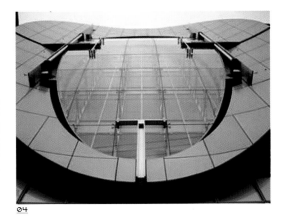

Gotham City's gothic surrounds were the perfect stomping ground to reintroduce *Batman*'s brooding psyche. A world of shadows, of stylized sets glinting in moonlight. Tim Burton's brutalist, steroidal realignment of the *Batman* legend was most successful due largely to the inspired production design of Anton Furst. The production team used the tone of the DC's *Dark Knight* comics as reference.

The heightened sense of a hazy metropolis belching smoke from the streets was inspired by Andreas Feininger's pictures of New York's buildings in the 1940s. Adding to this overall impression, the kind of detailing evident in the architecture of Japan's Shin Takamatsu, with its bold geometric cut-outs, curves, and hard edges, added a more contemporary twist. Echoes of the oval of the college in Fukuoka, the parasitic metal roof welded onto the ARK-Nishina Dental Clinic, Kyoto, or the formalist turrets atop Kirin Plaza, Osaka, all make their way into the film's backlot-built sets.

"*Blade Runner* was consciously avoided as a reference," says Art Director Nigel Phelps. "No one was allowed to watch it while we were designing the film and neon was shunned altogether!" [1] Furst's thirst for developing new styles evolved into what he called an "almost Dadaesque juxtaposition of styles." [2]

Furst commented at the time of production: "We've got an incredible anomaly of different styles. So we have Antonio Gaudí stretched into a skyscraper, and we've got Otto Wagner [1841–1918, a leading Viennese architect] locked onto brownstone buildings with fascist fronts on it, and [Isambard Kingdom] Brunel-type Victorian bridges... We really wanted to express the evil quality of Gotham City."

IMAGES

01 *Batman* was "definitely based in many ways on the worst aspects of New York," according to Production Designer, Furst.
02 Andreas Feininger's photographs epitomize Manhattan as Gotham.
03–04 Signature Shin Takamatsu motifs where incorporated on set.

[ SOURCES ]

[1] *Production Design & Art Direction* (SCREENCRAFT,) PETER ETTEDGUI (ROTOVISION, 1999)

[2] *Anton Furst, The Creator of Gotham's Urban Blight*, ADAM PIRANI (1990)

2004
2003
2002
2001
2000
1999
1998
1997
1996
1995
1994
1993
1992
1991
1990
1989
1988
1987
1986
1985
1984
1983
1982

Revolving around the construction of the Babylon Project, a renewal project in Tokyo Bay, *Patlabor* is the breakthrough animated movie that popularized the mecha genre and esthetic in the West. In an age of powerful digital effects, this genre is on the verge of cross-pollinating live-action special effects adaptations such as *Evangelion* (2006). Although sequels *Patlabor 2* (1993), and *WXIII: Patlabor 3* (2002), along with Mamoru's feature adaptation of the manga *Ghost in the Shell* (1995) are more complete, better films, the simplicity of the original templates the pared-back, introspective, sci-fi elements evident in Oshii's oeuvre.

The action centers around rogue Labors (giant humanoid robots controlled by an internal operator, generally used for construction) and the development of artificial islands and other constructions in Tokyo Bay. The special police division have co-opted this technology to create Patlabors, which are pressed into service to aid investigations.

*Patlabor* is set in 1999, a very near future at the time of the film's production—only the mecha technology of the Labors, surrounding computer machinery and construction are that different from the present. This subtlest of science fiction plays as an indictment of Japanese culture that, during this period, was rushing into material access, buoyed by the unsustainable "bubble" economy. The emphasis on a throwaway culture, of urban decay and ruin, the demolishing of historic districts, alongside extravagant new development in the form of the massive Babylon Project tower—a hi-tech Ark in Tokyo Bay—contrast and illustrate the issue in no uncertain terms. Oshii's feature is a thoughtful examination of urban development and architectural changes in our metropolises. As one character says, "That's modern-day Tokyo for you: skyscrapers and smog."

Director Mamoru Oshii has confessed fantasizing as a young boy about living alone in a deserted, post-apocalyptic city. Throughout his work, he returns constantly to technology and how humans respond to this, particularly with reference to artificially intelligent technology, feeling it is an issue society needs to address before it's too late. "As well as Japanese animation, technology has a huge influence on Japanese society and also Japanese novels. I think it's because before, people tended to think that ideology or religion were the things that actually changed people, but it's been proven that that's not the case. I think nowadays, technology has been proven to be the thing that's actually changing people. So in that sense, it's become a theme in Japanese culture." [1]

# PATLABOR

**FILM**

**VISUAL EFFECTS**

+ **ANIMATION PRODUCTION: STUDIO DEEN, HEADGEAR**

**CREDITS**
DIRECTOR: **MAMORU OSHII**
SCREENPLAY: **KAZUNORI ITO**
FROM THE MANGA OF: **MASAMI YUUKI**
MECHANICAL DESIGN: **YUTAKA IZUBUCHI**
CHARACTER DESIGN: **AKEMI TAKADA**
PRODUCERS: **SHIN UNOZAWA, TARO MAKI, MAKATO KUBO**

01

02

03

04

05

06

07

IMAGES

01—07 *Patlabor*'s Tokyo is a mix of the traditional and
modern with futuristic accoutrements.

【 SOURCE 】

[1] ONION A/V CLUB, TASHA ROBINSON (09/2004)

2004
2003
2002
2001
2000
1999
1998
1997
1996
1995
1994
1993
1992
1991
1990
1989
1988
1987
1986
1985
1984
1983
1982

Paul Verhoeven's vision of memory implants, interplanetary spies, and terraforming, is a compelling adventure caper based on Philip K. Dick's science fiction story. Consistently seen as one of the best unproduced scripts in Hollywood before it was greenlit thanks to Schwarzenegger's star power, *Total Recall* is an audience-pleasing spectacular. Zealots of "hard" science fiction may be shocked by the inaccuracies in its science, but for those who want to follow Quaid from a 2084 Earth to a Mars Colony of mutants, ancient alien races and architecture, it is a dizzying ride courtesy of Rekall, Inc (the memory implanters where the action kicks in).

A film with an excess of verve, *Total Recall*'s plot is as delirious as its detailed production design, courtesy of William Sandell and his art department. Schwarzenegger's character careers through gray urban modernist Earth, to the red-hued encapsulated colony outpost of Mars, taking in the ghetto district of Venusville, federal mines, and of course a massive alien terraforming device. The visualization of the mining outpost and this ancient ½ million years old reactor inside the Federal Colony's pyramid mine is achieved through minatures and matte painting, alongside physical sets. Verhoeven apparently got the idea for the hanging rods of the alien reactor when he threw an architectural book on the floor in frustration and a picture of skyscrapers landed upside down.
>>>

IMAGES

01 The Martian outpost is achieved through a combination of miniatures, mattes, and physical sets.

# TOTAL RECALL

| FILM | VISUAL EFFECTS |
|---|---|
| | + DREAMQUEST (DQI) |

CREDITS
DIRECTOR: PAUL VERHOEVEN
PRODUCTION DESIGNER: WILLIAM SANDELL
SCREENPLAY: RONALD SHUSETT, DAN O BANNON, JON POVILL
SCREEN STORY: RONALD SHUSETT, DAN O BANNON, GARY GOLDMAN
BASED ON THE SHORT STORY: "WE CAN REMEMBER IT FOR YOU WHOLESALE"
BY PHILIP K. DICK
PRODUCERS: BUZZ FEITSHANS, RONALD SHUSETT

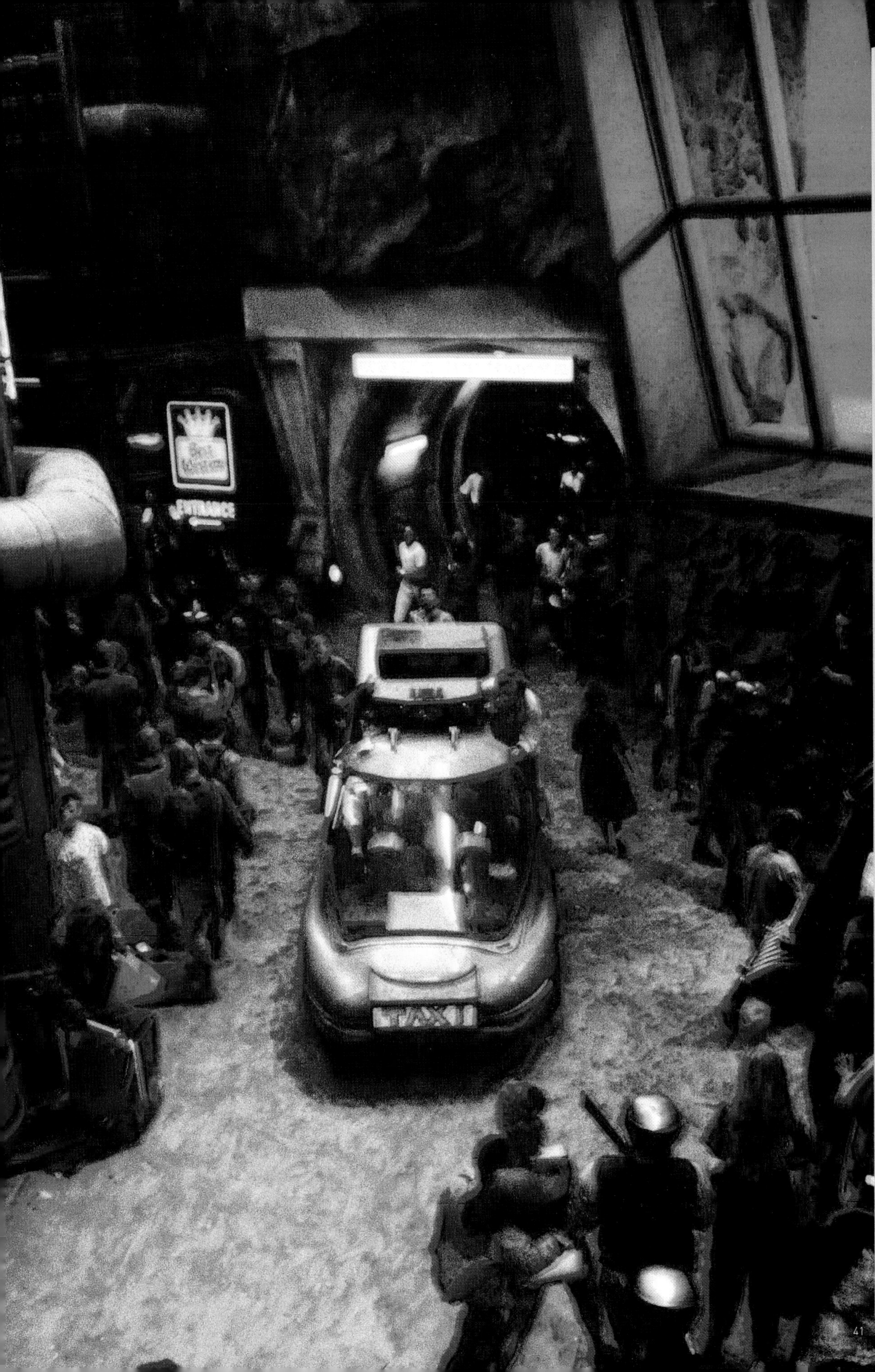
ENTRANCE
TAXI

2004
2003
2002
2001
2000
1999
1998
1997
1996
1995
1994
1993
1992
1991
**1990**
1989
1988
1987
1986
1985
1984
3

01

### IMAGES

01  William Sandell's outstanding production design resulted in breathtaking Mars locations, such as Venusville.

02–03  Miniatures were used extensively for Martian colony shots from the planet surface.

04  A miniatures set being modified.

04

Verhoeven's high-concept ultra-violence was controversial on the movie's release, but he still manages to include allusions to fighting against inequality, as he does with his other films. He would argue his work satirizes and comments on the very things they are attacked for promoting.

The film used minimal digital techniques (the walking x-ray machine, being one of the most high profile of the time). Sandell's masterly use of sets creates convincing flavors of both a future Earth and a Mars colony. "Actors leaning on two-by-fours in front of a green screen makes it hard to get great performances," he states in relation to the crop of 'digital backlot' motion pictures. "You never want to say never, but no director of any worth is going to go for a wholly digital/virtual approach unless they have other reasons. It diminishes performances. There's a feeling of disconnect during the filming, and for the audiences. I don't buy too much trickery."[1]

Sandell's caution over the slavish devotion to CG is well meant. While an immense boon to a genre which lives on the spectacularly imagined, the software tools and modelling mindset can tunnel artists into a groupthink approach, smoothing out the rough edges and "creative mistakes" that can move the medium forward. "I'm not a luddite, I think this stuff is amazing," he says referring to the advances in digital effects, "but I like to keep a critical distance."

【 SOURCE 】

[1] WILLIAM SANDELL, ORIGINAL INTERVIEW, MATT HANSON (9/2004)

2004
2003
2002
2001
2000
1999
1998
1997
1996
1995
1994
1993
1992
1991
1990
1989
1988
1987
1986
1985
1984
1983
1982

⌀1

# ALIEN³

**FILM**

**CREDITS**
DIRECTOR: **DAVID FINCHER**
PRODUCTION DESIGNER: **NORMAN REYNOLDS**
SCREENPLAY: **DAVID GILER, WALTER HILL, LARRY FERGUSON**
STORY: **VINCENT WARD**
VISUAL EFFECTS SUPERVISOR: **RICHARD EDLUND**
PRODUCERS: **GORDON CARROLL, DAVID GILER, WALTER HILL**

A caustic classic, *Alien³* is an underrated instalment in the most influential science fiction horror franchise of them all. Ripley's EEV (Emergency Escape Vehicle) is ejected from the spaceship Sulaco and crashlands on Fiorina "Fury" 161, a prison planet—the perfect setting to extend the bleak, industrial, decaying vision of the *Alien* films.

Director David Fincher's wish was for a more mechanical world to that originally envisioned. A world where everything communicated that this was a run-down wreck of a planet, rusted, broken, waste-ridden. *Alien³*, even more than its predecessors is a template for the survival horror genre, exceptionally influential in the videogame world, but also increasingly popular in science fiction. Fincher's vision was too ahead of its time, too unremittingly bleak and downbeat compared to the maxed-out machismo of James Cameron's *Aliens* (1986) actioner, or even Ridley Scott's 1979 original gothic space chiller.
>>>

IMAGES

01 *Alien³* was set in an unremittingly bleak environment, an extension of the franchise's unapologetically scuzzy esthetic.
02 *Alien* architecture embodies the signature style of the series, the bio-organic designs of H.R. Giger.

2004
2003
2002
2001
2000
1999
1998
1997
1996
1995
1994
1993
1992
1991
1990
1989
1988
1987
1986
1985
1984
1983
1982

01

The grotesque alien architecture adapted by
the Swiss artist H.R. Giger so famously for *Alien*,
was so resonant due to its sheer exoticism, the
fact it alluded so creepily to sexual organs and
reproductive imagery. And while we don't get
any of the *Alien* environments in the third film,
this generates an even more uneasy
atmosphere—it is closer to our reality, firmly
set in an extension of the world we live in.
And *Alien*[3] still manages to extend the analogy
of reproduction—the uterine passages of the
Refinery's tunnels are a sinister setting for
the inmates to hunt and be hunted.

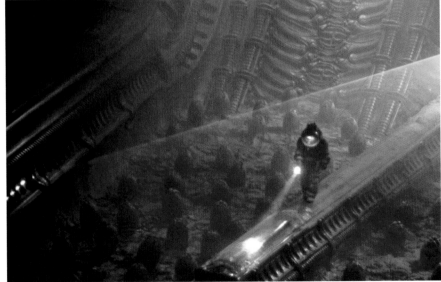

02

05

Despite the industrial nature of the Mineral
Ore Refinery, it was predominantly made out
of foam core and cardboard. Due to budgetary
and time constraints, miniatures used a forced
perspective that utilized more shadows to hide
the lack of building details. Still, the planet sets
are finely realized, conveying a claustrophobic,
oppressive environment. The texture of the
setting is aided by real-world construction.

Minimal CG was used throughout the film.
*Alien*³ was on the cusp of the digital revolution in
effects, and acts as a masterly set piece
advertising the best of physical set construction,
without computer-generated aids. Matte
paintings were used extensively to create the
exterior shots, even containing sly homages to
predecessors: a shot looking across the planet
surface filled with cranes has a deliberate
homage to *Blade Runner* (see page 18) painted in
the background—one of those Maya-inspired
pyramids can be made out in the distance.
>>>

2004
2003
2002
2001
2000
1999
1998
1997
1996
1995
1994
1993
**1992**
1991
1990
1989
1988
1987
1986
1985
1984
1983
1982

Ø1

*Alien*³ is remarkable as much for the missed opportunity to create a truly radical science fiction environment as it is for its ability to extend the glorious alien environments in its heritage to resolutely grim tone, set in a murky, claustrophobic, industrial complex.

The film had an extended and troubled production. Before Fincher was parachuted in at a late stage to resuscitate production, New Zealander Vincent Ward had elaborated a unique and medieval vision of a three-mile-wide wooden space planet, Arceon. A world straight out of Hieronymous Bosch where, according to Ward, "Ripley wandered into the tenth Century." Arceon would have been a monastic colony that rejected all excess technology, floating in space, replete with wooden cathedrals, windmills, wheat fields, and foundries—everything that was needed to keep them self-sufficient. It would have been an exhilarating mix of the futuristic and the feudal. Falling under the weight of its ambition, the scenario was brought back to a more recognizable one by Fincher, but crucial elements such as religion, the foundry, and tunnels as de facto catacombs, were kept.

The macabre mise-en-scène of the *Alien* series has never been bettered, and *Alien*³ contributes to that with fervor. This is the enduring appeal of a science fiction franchise which is anti-futuristic, that tells us looking to the stars, searching out beyond the sky, could get us into a whole heap of trouble.

IMAGES

01 *Alien: Resurrection* included flooded environments.
02 *Aliens* features a Queen Alien nesting ground.

2004
2003
2002
2001
2000
1999
1998
1997
1996
**1995**
1994
1993
1992
1991
1990
1989
1988
1987
1986
1985
1984
1983
1982

Ø1

# MEMORIES

**FILM**

Ø2

Katsuhiro Otomo's portmanteau film, inspired by his own graphic short stories, experiments with animated styles and storytelling to create a mesmerizing sci-fi triptych. The progressive animé films seem entirely unrelated—apart from exploring different sub-genres of science fiction—differing wildly in both presentation and tone. Otomo, Koji Morimoto, and Tensai Okamura—three masterful animation directors—blend exquisitely drawn animation enhanced with CG in seamless ways.

*Magnetic Rose*, Morimoto's opener, is an elegiac space opera. Somber and reflective in tone, it concerns the crew of the Corona, an orbiting spaceship that collects space junk. In their orbit they find a massive, derelict, haunted space vessel shaped like a rose, and inside find it was once home to an opera diva. Floating metals on the outside of the vessel, with predominant hues of muted rust and brown, lead to interiors inspired by Venetian architecture. As they venture deeper inside, the marble and colonnades give way to a more sinister organicism, and the H.R. Giger interiors of Alien. A science fiction where *Madame Butterfly* meets *Solaris* (see page 96), *Magnetic Rose* has an eerie, paranormal poetry that is unforgettable.

Okamura's second chapter, *Stink Bomb*, adds slapstick relief. A cautionary sci-fi comedy set in near-contemporary Tokyo, protagonist Tanaka Nobue unwittingly becomes a bio-weapon by taking a pill from the stylish modernist confines of the government laboratory where he works. On finding his colleagues dead in the lab, he rushes to Tokyo with the data, oblivious to the fact that the drug has reacted with his DNA to produce a lethal stench. Playing out along the transit system toward the megalopolis, the country's military line up against this human skunk. Destroyed vistas have their echo in live-action equivalents such as *28 Days Later* (2002), and its antecedent, *The Omega Man* (1971). An absurdist warning on bio-terrorism and genetic modification, this chapter is firmly from the *Dr. Strangelove* camp of sci-fi.

**CREDITS**
DIRECTORS: **KATSUHIRO OTOMO, KOJI MORIMOTO, TENSAI OKAMURA**
PRODUCTION DESIGNERS: **YUJI IKEHATA, MITSUO KOSEKI, AKIRA YAMAKAWA**
SCREENPLAY: **SATOSHI KON, KATSUHIRO OTOMO**
PRODUCER: **SHIGERU WATANABE**

IMAGES

Ø1 Okamura's modernist *Stink Bomb* laboratory.
Ø2 Archigram's Walking City is reimagined in Otomo's retro-futuristic *Cannon Fodder*.
Ø3–Ø4 *Cannon Fodder*'s satirical City as giant weapon.
Ø5–Ø6 The interiors of *Magnetic Rose* veer between Venetian and alien.
Ø7–Ø8 Steam-age constructivist architectural detailing.

03

07

04

08

05

*Cannon Fodder* is Otomo's finale. A sketchy tale of an industrial city, seemingly modeled on those of Cold War-era Russia, with workers who specialize in destruction not production. Otomo's first animé proper post-*Akira*, *Cannon Fodder* veers into totally different territory from *Akira*'s stunning rendering of neo-Tokyo. Here, Otomo has conjured up an Orwellian state reminiscent of *1984*, in which a totalitarian society is geared to servicing the Howitzers which dominate its skyline. Almost every building is topped by a massive cannon. The internal and societal structure set up to service these gigantic barrels with enormous caliber shells firing over a wasteland to hit an unseen enemy's hidden and moving city. The film commingles the architecture of Alexei Shchusev and his Stalinist classicism, with Constructivist propaganda à la Alexander Rodchenko, and the avant-gardism of Ron Herron and Archigram's Walking Cities— Futurism given a retro-Constructivist twist.

06

2004
2003
2002
2001
2000
1999
1998
1997
1996
**1995**
1994
1993
1992
1991
1990
1989
1988
1987
1986
1985
1984
1983
1982

# THE CITY OF LOST CHILDREN

**FILM**

| VISUAL EFFECTS |
| --- |
| + DUBOI |

Ø1

A highly stylized adult fairy tale, the French feature film *The City of Lost Children* is a tour de force of art direction. Managing to combine the spirits of both Jules Verne and George Méliès, this long-gestating project (Caro, the film's co-director, stated that it took them 14 years to get it on to the screen) deserves its place among the work that clearly influenced it: French science fiction and fantasy literary tradition.

The harbor city featured in the film, dank nearby slums, and villain Krank's offshore laboratory could be lifted straight from one of Verne's stories. The sea rig itself might easily have been the base for Captain Nemo's Nautilus submarine from the book, *20,000 Leagues Under the Sea*. "It's a retro future, a former future," comments Caro. "The esthetic of the film is very Jules Verne... also Frankenstein's laboratory, with the bolts."[1]

The science fiction fantasy has a glossy exoticism which belies its superficially everyday settings. The world's heightened reality benefits from the atmospheric cinematography of Darius Khondji. Vivid red and greens suffuse the damp surfaces of the sets, while the camera twists and winds over slick bricks and riveted metal. The production design deliberately highlights the artifice of the enterprise. These are storybook pages from a parallel universe come to life, not simulacra of the future.

>>>

**CREDITS**
DIRECTOR: **MARC CARO, JEAN-PIERRE JEUNET**
PRODUCTION DESIGNERS: **MARC CARO, JEAN RABASSE**
SCREENPLAY: **GILLES ADRIEN, JEAN-PIERRE JEUNET, MARC CARO**
DIGITAL SPECIAL EFFECTS: **PITOF**
PRODUCER: **CLAUDIE OSSARD**

IMAGES

01–03  The feature has a highly stylized look, highlighting the distressed harbor area with pervading hues of greens, browns, and reds that are a motif of the production design.

2004
2003
2002
2001
2000
1999
1998
1997
1996
**1995**
1994
1993
1992
1991
1990
1989
1988
1987
1986
1985
1984
1983
1982

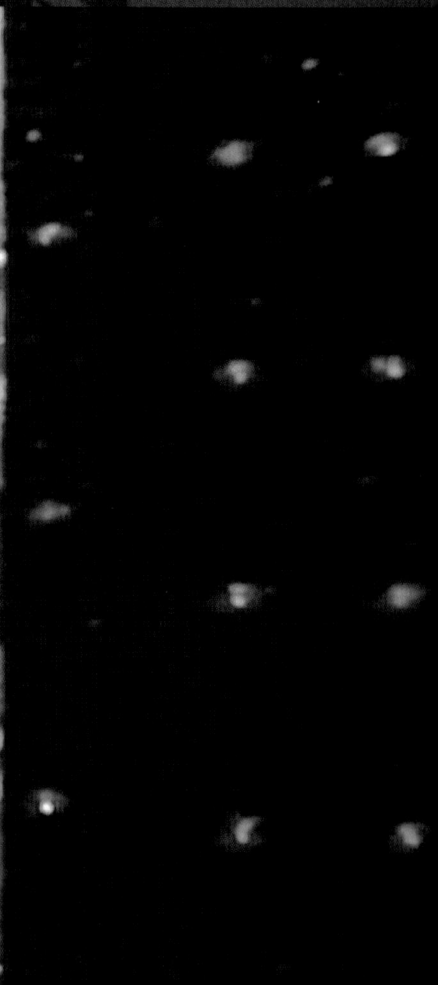

03

**IMAGES**

01-03  The offshore floating rig is archetypally creepy, inspired by Jules Verne crossed with Frankenstein's lab.

"IT'S A RETRO FUTURE, A FORMER FUTURE. THE ESTHETIC OF THE FILM IS VERY JULES VERNE... ALSO FRANKENSTEIN'S LABORATORY, WITH THE BOLTS." MARC CARO

Jeunet and Caro's dreamworld has strange cyborg Cyclops stealing children for evil scientist Krank to leech them of their dreams. The adventure is an elaborate dystopian vision, replete with fabulous grotesques, reminiscent of a Diane Arbus shoot. *The City of Lost Children* is science fiction retold by the Brothers Grimm, or Charles Perrault–it brings the cruel and disturbing back into the realm of childhood.

Caro: "In every way, in this film, our vision of dreams is not at all realistic. We've read all the books about dreams, their significance; but, while it was thoroughly interesting, it wasn't necessary to take it into consideration for the story that we wanted to tell. One takes a greater risk in the realm of fairy tales than in dreams, in the proper sense. So we went in that direction, letting our imagination manifest itself."

**[ SOURCE ]**

**[1]** "A CONVERSATION WITH JEAN-PIERRE JEUNET AND MARC CARO," ALAIN SCHLOCKOFF & CATHY KARANI (11/1995)

2004
2003
2002
2001
2000
1999
1998
1997
1996
**1995**
1994
1993
1992
1991
1990
1989
1988
1987
1986
1985
1984
1983
1982

**FILM**

# JOHNNY MNEMONIC

+ SONY PICTURES IMAGEWORKS, FANTASY II FILM, BRAID MEDIA ARTS

VISUAL EFFECTS

"I SEE THE PRESENT AS BEING VAGUELY DYSTOPIAN, AND VAGUELY UTOPIAN, AND THE FUTURE AS BEING MUCH LIKE THAT BUT WITH THE VOLUME TURNED UP."
ROBERT LONGO

**CREDITS**
DIRECTOR: **ROBERT LONGO**
PRODUCTION DESIGNER: **NILO RODIN-JAMERO**
WRITTEN BY: **WILLIAM GIBSON**
PRODUCERS: **ARNON MILCHAN, DON CARMODY**

What William Gibson foresaw as a "fable for the information age,"[1] a feature-length adaptation of his short story about a data courier inhabiting the cyberpunk near future of 2021, is a flawed but distinctive movie. Johnny embeds encrypted data into his brain to securely transport the stolen information to another location without the use of networks. In doing so, he must negotiate internal and external terrains (a visualization of cyberspace, and of a future corporate-controlled urban dystopia).

*Johnny Mnemonic* is both banal action movie and an intriguingly disjointed visual melange; something to do with the fact that it was originally a quirky art film budgeted at $1.5 million, which became a $30 million job. As the budget spiralled, demands for a straightforward "cyberspace" action thriller with more cyberspace-style CG graphics became stronger. Artist-turned-filmmaker Robert Longo's original idea of an "edgy, black-and-white science fiction film" was fatefully wounded by Hollywood re-editing, but the extended Japanese version of the film goes some way to being closer to the Director and Writer's intentions.

The quirkily familiar but unreal environment remains. Director Robert Longo, part of the notable 1980s generation of appropriation artists, made his name reprocessing mass-media imagery via disjunctive materials and methods, and adapting them into fine art. This background comes through in the look and feel of the whole film. He wanted the film to take on a: "Weird Haiku effect... I tried to use the same jerkiness or between-space that much of my art works dealt with in the past. Collision of styles and filmic techniques were my tools. And since the film was about memory, the images we made quoted movies, and the memories of movies, much like my earlier work. I would make reference to other movies: *Touch of Evil* (1958), *Alphaville* (1965), *Sweet Smell of Success* (1957), Japanese cartoons, *The Conformist* (1970). Hollywood understands that language, just not in an ironic way."[2]

>>>

IMAGES

01  *Johnny Mnemonic* in Lotek Heaven.
02  Central Beijing.
03  The Lotek Bridge, cut off from advancing technology.
04  Underside of the abandoned bridge, the Lotek base.
05  The Bridge, retrofitted with junk defenses.

2004
2003
2002
2001
2000
1999
1998
1997
1996
**1995**
1994
1993
1992
1991
1990
1989
1988
1987
1986
1985
1984
1983
1982

Ø1

Ø2

The film follows Johnny from a corporate-hued Central Beijing to the Free City of Newark, through environments which become more plausible every day. The budding of a thousand skyscrapers in China's booming cities, and the sprawl of mega-cities such as Sao Paulo and its unofficial extensions through the favelas, are reflected in this alternative future, only five degrees away from the present. The film's equivalent to the favelas is a bridge populated by a tribe of Loteks, a societal underclass who have reclaimed abandoned industrial freight containers, welded scrap, cables, and girders, to create, as their leader J-Bone states, "Heaven built outta straight-world junk." The bridge is a motif that looms larger in the author's imagination through his later Bridge trilogy of books. *Johnny Mnemonic* successfully transfers Gibson's core motif of junk-tech, where "the street makes its own uses for things."

Trash is recoded to work as building code. The way the bridge–an amalgam of this trash–is made up of this material evokes the Japanese cyberpunk feature, *Tetsuo: Iron Man* (1988). In *Tetsuo*, the protagonist cybernetically mutates, attracting metal through magnetic force, creating a weird, hybrid skeletal structure. Gibson says, "This kind of environment is something I come back to over and over in my work. Seeing one constructed, full-size, in much greater detail, much higher resolution... It looked like a place. A very real place."[1]

Longo has described his work as existing between the movie and the monument. His "Men in the Cities" installation presented studies of office workers interspersed with cast aluminum reliefs of brutal architectural forms. The film is more obsessed with these forms sculpting the space than it is with characterization. The Bridge's control room is dominated by a giant television tower of flickering video streams and a jump seat from which to access the internal geometries and topographies of this future world. Johnny sits in this seat, putting on a data helmet, to jack into and negotiate visualizations of information related to real-world locations. This dataworld is satisfyingly electronic, semi-abstract, and glossy compared to the scuzzy, run-down industrialness of the Free City.

The film faithfully reproduces Gibson's milieu more successfully than the star of the cyberpunk sci-fi genre, *The Matrix* (1999). Although *Johnny Mnemonic* is no way near as satisfying a film, this book is about architecture—as such, the visual overload provided by Longo is an individually peculiar one. The duality between the corporate and non-corporate spaces and the ambiguity of the environments is something which chimes well with Gibson's vision: "I see the present as being vaguely dystopian, and vaguely utopian, and the future as being much like that but with the volume turned up. I think utopia and dystopia are historical concepts at this point, but we just haven't realized it. Somewhere we crossed the line, and now we're in this disoriented point."[3]

IMAGES

Ø1 Sony Pictures Imageworks and Braid media were tasked with creating cyberspace. Frames took up to five hours to render on a 150mhz Indigo2 box. An Alias Research SGI rendering farm, and a SGI Black Onyx computer completed the at-the-time cutting-edge visual effects.
Ø2–Ø3 Longo's conception of junk-tech permeates the movie, echoing his own video sculptures.
Ø4–Ø7 Braid used custom plug-ins for 3D studio, The Valis Group's MetaFlo', and Boris Tsikanovsky's Realtime. Creating animated maps and textures was an arduous process, requiring frame-by-frame manipulation of TIFF files.

04

05

06

07

[ SOURCES ]

[1] "REMEMBERING JOHNNY", *Wired magazine*, VOL 3.06
[2] DISCUSSION WITH ROBERT LONGO BY MICHAEL
COHEN, ARTCOMMOTION.COM `
[3] "INVENTOR OF CYBERSPACE STEPS BACK TO THE
PRESENT", WILLIAM GIBSON INTERVIEW BY KARLIN
LILLINGTON, IRISH TIMES, 25 APRIL 2003

2004
2003
2002
2001
2000
1999
1998
1997
1996
1995
1994
1993
1992
1991
1990
1989
1988
1987
1986
1985
1984
1983
1982

+ DIGITAL DOMAIN, USING SOFTIMAGE, ARETE, SIDE EFFECTS' PRISMS, RENDERMAN, AND PROPRIETARY SOFTWARE.

VISUAL EFFECTS

# THE FIFTH ELEMENT

FILM

*The Fifth Element* is an exuberantly Gallic take on the future, directed by Luc Besson—a comic-book science fiction adventure made real. His regular collaborator, production designer Dan Weil, created an environment based on New York, fast-forwarded to the future. He used artists from the science fiction comics Luc Besson was addicted to in his youth–Moebius and Jean-Claude Mézières—to create an idiosyncratic futurescape. Over a year, Besson's team systematically tackled the major elements of this future world—its transport (both on Earth and in space), interior design and exterior architecture, alongside the ubiquitous design inherent in future living.

Besson's overriding aim was to steer away from clichés of the genre. He wanted to build on traditional design (as can be seen with the flying New York cabs zipping between the skyscraper canyons of the future city). "By creating a little destruction, I'm creating life," states the movie's arch-villain, Zorg. This ebullient universe threatens to tear itself apart, it goes in so many creative directions. It sweeps away the rationalist design extensions of more serious sci-fi futures, and exchanges it for the sheer zest of imaginative excess.
>>>

01

CREDITS

DIRECTOR: **LUC BESSON**

PRODUCTION DESIGNERS: **DAN WEIL, JEAN-CLAUDE MÉZIÈRES**

VISUAL EFFECTS SUPERVISOR: **MARK STETSON**

STORY: **LUC BESSON**

SCREENPLAY: **LUC BESSON, ROBERT MARK KAMEN**

> "CITIES WILL EVOLVE IN THE FUTURE, BUT THEY WILL BUILD ON WHAT IS ALREADY THERE."
>
> DAN WEIL

02

IMAGES

01—02  The final composition of *The Fifth Element*'s spaceport, at the foot of what was once New York's Hudson River, differed little from the initial concept sketches.

2004
2003
2002
2001
2000
1999
1998
**1997**
1996
1995
1994
1993
1992
1991
1990
1989
1988
1987
1986
1985
1984
1983
1982

01

02

"As a Production Designer, my role in this process was as much editorial as creative," states Weil in the book, *Production Design and Art Direction* [1]. "Without dictating a design style, I wanted to make the design colloquial and ensure that we didn't entirely lose touch with reality; if you feature a flying car, the audience want to understand how it works. If you don't put a big engine under it, for example, they won't accept the idea. I also wanted to avoid sci-fi design clichés. Contemporary design is about simplifying the lines and operational features of the technology we live with; and yet most futuristic design one sees in the cinema complicates everything–there are flashing lights, dozens of buttons and switches, smoke. Getting the level of technology right was essential to me. We sought to avoid making every aspect of the design hyper-modern; we keep the basic body of the New York cab, for example."

03

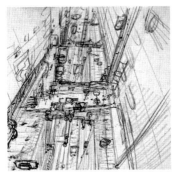

04

The design has a wry humor about it. Initially, *The Fifth Element*'s hero, Korben Dallas (played by Bruce Willis), drives a familiar-looking NYC Yellow cab with an anti-gravity upgrade. In fact, the skies are filled with flying vehicles darting through a thrillingly chaotic New York City, where skyscraper canyons descend into smog and extend into the stratosphere. These relate directly to Mézières' early conception of the city, where future elements are bolted on to the familiar. *The Fifth Element*'s garish comic book colors and weird science were a refreshing antidote to the faded future noir copies of *Blade Runner*'s landscape of rain-soaked gritty urbanism that had become a standard view of a cinematic future throughout the 1990s.

"The work Luc and his production designer Dan Weil did on the New York cityscape had a very specific aim," explains Mark Stetson, the Visual Effects Supervisor (who was, coincidentally, the chief model maker of the miniatures sets and Hades-like landscape of *Blade Runner*.) Stetson oversaw over 200 digitally created or enhanced shots in the movie. "Traditionally, New York is characterized by its grid-like, rectilinear street layout. Curving streets and T-intersections would normally be used to constrain the view, so as to fit onto a model stage in miniature, or into a live-action screen for that matter. Luc and Dan didn't want to do this. They wanted to depict New York as they saw it—a European rather than an American view."

>>>

IMAGES

01–04 Mézières' New York bolts future elements on to the familiar landscape.

2004
2003
2002
2001
2000
1999
1998
**1997**
1996
1995
1994
1993
1992
1991
1990
1989
1988
1987
1986
1985
1984
1983
1982

Ø1

Luc's photographic style for this and many other films is very centered, with one-point perspectives fixed right on the cross hairs of the camera lens. And that reflects somewhat the difference between the American comic book tradition and the French graphic artist heritage, the latter being the source for the look and design of this film. In this film, we have one-point perspectives centerd down the middle of the streets, with a vanishing point to infinity. And we look down those streets forever." [2]

To create these rich vistas, Stetson and his crew used a combination of miniatures in the fore- and mid-ground, with digital 2D matte-painted backgrounds, and a CG layer of buzzing sky traffic. They created comprehensive miniatures to reproduce the level of detail Besson was after, while sticking to Weil's mantra: "Cities will evolve in the future, but they will build on what is already there."

Eric Hanson, one of the artists at Digital Domain, was able to build virtual sets within a digital environment to enhance the use of miniatures, riffing off of Mézières conceptualization of a future Earth sucked dry. The oceans have retreated, and the Hudson and East rivers surrounding the City have long disappeared, "establishing the island of Manhattan on a high plateau reminiscent of the Acropolis." [3] This leaves Brooklyn Bridge hundreds of meters in the air, while buildings cling to its foundations and populate the riverbed below.

"This changed the notion of a single street and ground plane for circulation", explains Hanson. "So hovering craft were envisioned to roam into stratified layers throughout the verticality." In such a way, the production design evolved away from the commonplace vision in science fiction of supercharged skyscraper structures, and "towering megastructures." Mézières had populated his concept drawings with details such as vertical subways clattering up and down the sides of buildings, and this type of detail adds a deeper filigree to proceedings.

[ SOURCES ]

[1] *Production Design & Art Direction* (SCREENCRAFT) , PETER ETTEDGUI (ROTOVISION, 1999)

[2] LUC BESSON ARTICLE, MARK STETSON INTERVIEW, NIGEL FLOYD, *Sight & Sound* (1997)

[3] "DIGITAL FICTION: NEW REALISM IN FILM ARCHITECTURE," ERIC HANSON, *Architecture & Film II*, ED. BOB FEAR (WILEY ACADEMY, 2000)

02

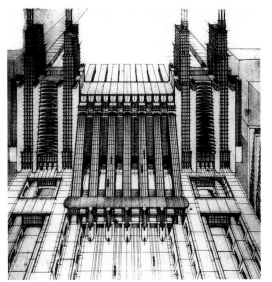

03

To complete *The Fifth Element*'s cluttered urban environment, motion control cameras moved through 1:24 scale sets, and this movement data was then exported to track and produce the 3D animation of sky traffic zipping around the City. Key reference points in constructing this new NYC included Metabolist-inspired clusters of modular apartment from the 1960s, and Antonio Sant'Elia's futurist architectural ideas. These were incorporated into the design in the way buildings were interconnected, into a multi-level mass of aerial walkways, plazas, and towers.

The film's most important legacy? To extend the idea cinematic futures don't have to be dark and dystopic, industrial or minimilist, sober or horrific. Ultimately, the day-glo "pop" originality of *The Fifth Element*'s production design is the deciding factor in elevating this movie beyond its pulp narrative and throwaway origins, into classic contemporary sci-fi.

04

IMAGES

01 Towering megastructures populate a futuristic Manhattan traversed by hovering cabs.
02–03 The futurist architecture of the Italian Antonio Sant'Elia was an inspiration for *The Fifth Element*'s cityscapes. Notably, between 1912-1914, his studies of the Città Nuova (New City), conceiving of a new age of urbanism, were highly influential.
04 Manhattan high-rise models referencing the design of Sant'Elia.

2004
2003
2002
2001
2000
1999
1998
1997
1996
1995
1994
1993
1992
1991
1990
1989
1988
1987
1986
1985
1984
1983
1982

02

# STARSHIP TROOPERS

**FILM**

**VISUAL EFFECTS**

TIPPETT STUDIO, SONY PICTURES IMAGEWORKS, AMALGAMATED DYNAMICS, ILM, BOSS FILM, MASS ILLUSIONS, COMPOUND EYE, BANNED FROM THE RANCH, VISUAL CONCEPT ENGINEERING, PIXEL LIBERATION FRONT, KEVIN YAGHER PRODUCTIONS.

01

Director Paul Verhoeven takes Robert Heinlein's hard science fiction novel glorifying military service and morals and turns it on its head. A veteran of sci-fi, having already completed *Robocop* (1987) and *Total Recall* (1990, see page 40), Verhoeven wanted to tackle the genre utilizing the "hard edge of war." *Starship Troopers* hones a style he used on *Robocop* satirizing media coverage and the contemporary language of advertising that is used to sell us everything from foodstuffs to philosophy and politics. The "Countdown to Victory" segment of the film was inspired by the Gulf War, which was going on when the project started. It is meant to directly evoke the CNN coverage of the first Gulf War.

"This whole movie is modeled on American propaganda films of World War II, and also the Third Reich," Verhoeven has stated, making it very clear that this film was meant as an antidote to the moral ambiguity sweeping through cinema at the time. The intention was to have a simple reading and moral view where the bad guys wear black or are alien arachnids.

The propaganda is foregrounded as *Starship Trooper*'s first image is of a Federal Network broadcast that continues to intersperse the movie and chronicles the battle between Earth and the Klendathu arachnids. Over 500 visual effects in the movie were predominantly used to create the performance of swarms of alien spiders, but the Director's subversive eye also has time to parody a world turned into a bland, totalitarian paradise. Render farms using After Effects were put on overtime to create the teeming masses of insects.

**CREDITS**
DIRECTOR: **PAUL VERHOEVEN**
PRODUCTION DESIGNER: **ALLAN CAMERON**
VISUAL EFFECTS SUPERVISORS: **PHIL TIPPETT, SCOTT E. ANDERSON**
SCREENPLAY: **EDWARD NEUMEIER**
ADAPTED FROM THE BOOK: **ROBERT A HEINLEIN**
PRODUCERS: **JON DAVISON, ALAN MARSHALL**

03

04

Mark Sullivan of Compound Eye oversaw 23 digital matte painting shots for the movie. For the planetary settlements and outposts, they used photographic elements alongside blowing dust and miniature windmills, then compositing in live-action humans to aid the illusion of realism.[1] Besides the utilitarian future military environments, clean and metallic, they also created an affluent Buenos Aires in before and after shots (it is destroyed as part of the interplanetary war). The environments on Earth are neutral and modern, a textbook international style amply demonstrated by the LA Convention Center stepping in as the Federal transport hub, the jumping off point for the new military recruits as they begin their journey.

The models of the space fleet, battle station, and planetary outposts took more than a year to craft. These models, up to eight feet long in some cases, were then enhanced with digital effects to add lighting and surface activity. Verhoeven's presentation of *Star Wars*-influenced space opera combined with interplanetary warfare, modeled on the Allied landings at Normandy, subverts a teen actioner into a warped sci-fi satire.

THE MODELS OF THE SPACE FLEET, BATTLE STATION, AND PLANETARY OUTPOSTS TOOK OVER ONE YEAR TO CRAFT. THESE MODELS, UP TO EIGHT FEET LONG IN SOME CASES, WERE THEN ENHANCED WITH DIGITAL EFFECTS TO ADD LIGHTING AND SURFACE ACTIVITY.

IMAGES

01–02  The sleek cityscape of Buenos Aires, heavily influenced by modern day Singapore.
03  Models of Federation outposts took more than a year to prepare, and were a far cry from the 150 layers which were employed in the digitally composited invasion fleet sequence.
04  Going to war. An internal transport system at the Spaceport.

[ SOURCE ]

[1] *Starship Troopers*, VFXHQ.COM, TODD VAZIRI, 1997

2004
2003
2002
2001
2000
1999
**1998**
1997
1996
1995
1994
1993
1992
1991
1990
1989
1988
1987
1986
1985
1984
1983
1982

# DARK CITY

**FILM**   **VISUAL EFFECTS**

+   **DFILM SERVICES SYDNEY**

**CREDITS**
DIRECTOR: **ALEX PROYAS**
PRODUCTION DESIGNERS: **PATRICK TATOPOULOS, GEORGE LIDDLE**
STORY: **ALEX PROYAS**
SCREENPLAY: **ALEX PROYAS, LEM DOBBS, DAVID S. GOYER**
PRODUCERS: **ANDREW MASON, ALEX PROYAS**
VISUAL EFFECTS SUPERVISOR: **ARTHUR WINDUS**

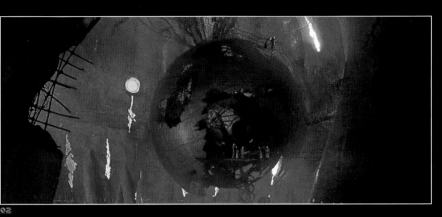

*Dark City* is an expressionistic mystery sci-fi set in the Stygian depths of space, replete with morphing buildings, mad scientists, and the ominous Strangers. The film's protagonist, Murdoch, wakes up to a world straight out of Edward Hopper's seminal painting, "Nighthawks." The film recreates a comic book Gotham which owes as much visually to the past as it does to the future—full of art deco automats, sleek, chromed vehicles, and clattering elevated trams. A future conceived by 1950s America, then taken over by an alien race. Director Alex Proyas' first science fiction film extended his dark, brooding comic book vision even further than his previous film, *The Crow* (1994).

In *Dark City*, Production Designer Patrick Tatopoulos was gifted a project where the sets and architecture were absolutely integral, and an important part of the narrative: "Because *Dark City* was close to my influences, I drew upon my formative stuff. What I like in art is when it's not too detailed. Powerful, dramatic statements, like the photorealism of Velasquez, or the Flemish real/surreal life-drawings of Bruegel and Bosch. I appreciate the expressionistic cinematography in the films of F.W. Murnau, Nosferatu's big shadows and strong whites. You build things to have that type of drama. *Dark City* gave the impression of that detail. I sketch in the same way, which gives the impression that you are putting in a lot more detail than you are through texture, giving it a busy look, and concentrating on selected elements. That was the way we designed *Dark City*. It maximized the budget we had in terms of what we could put in front of the camera. We gave the impression of this detail by concentrating on the elements in the foreground and making them as dramatic as possible. Brushstrokes in the background, detail in the foreground." [1]

>>>

IMAGES

01 The feature is filmed in deliberately lifeless color, with dense blacks and shadows throughout—a city in distress.
02–03 The Strangers congregate in subterranean control rooms where alien technology shapeshifts the planet.
04–05 Models were used alongside a street set, to define a mysterious film noir city.

2004
2003
2002
2001
2000
1999
**1998**
1997
1996
1995
1994
1993
1992
1991
1990
1989
1988
1987
1986
1985
**1984**
1983
1982

⊘1

⊘2

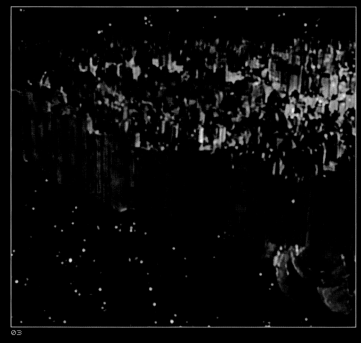

⊘3

A judicious use of miniatures, matte-painted backdrops, and sparing amounts of CG—until the tumultuous finale—combine to fashion an urban metropolis where, as arch-villain Mr. Hand states: "There's no escape. The city's ours, we made it... We fashioned this city on stolen memories. Different eras, different pasts, all rolled into one. Each night, we revise it—refine it—in order to learn."

With the Strangers using the world as a giant experiment, subterranean machines that focus their telepathic energy and alter the city are buried deep underground. In these chambers, the Strangers meet to reconfigure streets and avenues. Midnight sees the City being "tuned"— buildings grow from the ground, shift and warp into place.

Tatopoulos explains, "Sometimes, you get ideas from other jobs that aren't necessarily right for that film, but you file those away for later use. While working on Independence Day (1996), I watched them move building façades around. These fascias were being moved for different set-ups to give the impression of a bigger set and more buildings between filming. I thought to myself, 'I've got to use that,' so when it came to *Dark City*, where we have this morphing city, we used the idea of moving these set façades around as part of the theme."

*Dark City* evades the techno fantasies and future realities to stand out from other films in the genre by being something "other," stealing from film history to create an ode to the pleasures of the present. Proyas' fiction is an adult fantasy: "I like movies made for adolescent grown-ups. A few decades ago, it was still true that the golden age of science fiction readers was 12, but in my lifetime, it's become a mainstream genre." [2]

**[ SOURCES ]**

[1] PATRICK TATOPOULOS, ORIGINAL INTERVIEW, MATT HANSON (09/2004)

[2] "RISE OF THE MACHINES," CORY DOCTOROW, *Wired* (12/07/2004)

"WE GAVE THE IMPRESSION OF DETAIL BY CONCENTRATING ON THE ELEMENTS IN THE FOREGROUND AND MAKING THEM AS DRAMATIC AS POSSIBLE. BRUSHSTROKES IN THE BACKGROUND, DETAIL IN THE FOREGROUND." PATRICK TATOPOULOS

IMAGES

⊘1  A giant tuning machine underneath the city.
⊘2–⊘3  Beyond the city ramparts, nothing, in a film where there is only inner city and outer space.
⊘4  Spirals echo throughout the film's environments, from graffiti, to layout of districts, and the giant tuning machines.

2004
2003
2002
2001
2000
1999
1998
1997
1996
1995
1994
1993
1992
1991
1990
1989
1988
1987
1986
1985
1984
1983
1982

**FILM**

# STAR WARS: THE PHANTOM MENACE

**VISUAL EFFECTS**

+ **INDUSTRIAL LIGHT & MAGIC (ILM)**

To many people, science fiction film begins and ends with *Star Wars. Episode 1: The Phantom Menace* instigates the *Star Wars* saga, a space opera with mythical pretensions. This interplanetary adventure features chimerical human cities, death stars, and alien outposts alongside its star system-hopping intrigue and mammoth space battles. Among the dunes and droids, George Lucas has created the most popular and well-known world in science fiction. Despite its fantastical underpinnings, the environments we see at the start of the series in *Episode 1: The Phantom Menace* are quite familiar to us. Unlike the hard-edged, monumental, and often fascistic, architecture of the original *Star Wars* trilogy (Episodes 4-6)—chronologically set later than *Phantom Menace*, but actually filmed twenty years before—Lucas has been at pains to emphasize a more historical, less futuristic, style. So we get a sense of the eerily familiar, floating out of context, in a galaxy far, far away.

Doug Chiang, the design director for the prequel explains how the broad brushstrokes for the new trilogy were formulated: "There were many architectural influences. In order to make these new worlds believable, we had to anchor them in reality. We researched the eclectic architectural styles of Venice for Naboo. The Art Nouveau movement, particularly the work of Gaudí, was used for the Gungan City. Frank Lloyd Wright's Marin County Civic Center served as inspiration for the blue domes of Queen Amidala's palace. Hugh Ferriss and Albert Speers' monumental buildings influenced Coruscant. And lastly, Djerba architecture from Tunisia inspired the slave quarters of Tatooine."
>>>

*"I'VE FOUND THAT YOU SHOULD AVOID MAKING THINGS UP WITHOUT ANCHORING THEM TO A STRONG FOUNDATION BASED IN WORLD HISTORY."*
DOUG CHIANG

**CREDITS**
DIRECTOR: **GEORGE LUCAS**
PRODUCTION DESIGNER: **GAVIN BOCQUET**
WRITTEN BY: **GEORGE LUCAS**
VISUAL EFFECTS SUPERVISOR: **SCOTT SQUIRES**
DIRECTOR OF CONCEPT DESIGN: **DOUG CHIANG**
PRODUCER: **RICK MCCALLUM**

01

02

IMAGES

01 Coruscant, visible through the window, is a world covered by a vast megalopolis.
02 Lucas offers tantalizing glimpses of the cities of *Star Wars*, usually out of buildings and speeding craft.

2004
2003
2002
2001
2000
**1999**
1998
1997
1996
1995
1994
1993
1992
1991
1990
1989
1988
1987
1986
1985
1984
1983
1982

01

02

03

04

*Star Wars* can lay claim to having the most meticulously conceived and extensively developed production design of any film. And this comes through in the rich array of influences brought into play by the films. From Naboo to Degobah, Tatooine to Coruscant, Alderaan to Endor, the production design pillages our history to spin-off alien cultures and structures. "I've found that you should avoid making things up without anchoring them to a strong foundation based in world history," Chiang notes from experience.

Production Designer Gavin Bocquet created over 60 sets in *Episode 1*, spanning England, Italy, and Tunisia. These were predominantly built at Leavesden Studios in England, with the largest backlot in Europe available for construction. The Caserta Royal Palace near Naples stood in for the Queen Amidala's palace on Naboo. Other environments relied more on digital effects to be virtually created, as the trend toward more blue screen work carried into *Episode 2: Attack of the Clones* (2002). Notably, Coruscant was envisioned this way, a world whose entire surface consists of one vast megalopolis, and on which resides the Jedi Temple, and the Galactic Senate.

Both Naboo and Tatooine make up the primary locales of *The Phantom Menace*, alongside Coruscant. Naboo, a world as rural idyll, is blessed with the gloriously envisioned cities of Theed, and the underwater Gungan City. Tatooine, the most famous planet in the series, is an arid, free-spirited world on which can be found the colorful spaceport of Mos Eisley. All these metropolises are related to our reality, rather than the exotic planets in later instalments such as the Cloud City of Bespin, or the monumental cities in space of the Empire's Destroyer. The massed array of storm troopers we see parading in these space hangars echo the activity within the imposing chambers of Mussolini's Palazzo dei Congressi. *Star Wars'* breed of science fiction works so well because it taps into the architecturally familiar and makes it fantastic.

IMAGES

01 Classic *Star Wars* imagery takes the form of vast fascistic interiors brimming with Stormtroopers.
02 The Death Star is one of the most memorable images in science fiction film.
03 Braving the stylized trench of the Death Star.
04 The original *Star Wars* trilogy had design of a more vectoral and hard-edged nature.

2004

2003

2002

2001

2000

**1999**

1998

1997

1996

1995

1994

1993

1992

1991

1990

1989

1988

1987

1986

1985

1984

1983

1982

01

IMAGES

01  Although impossibly crude by today's standards, the futurescapes of *Star Wars* hold up remarkably well to scrutiny, due to the use of simple striking forms, and judicious use of surface lighting effects.

2004
2003
2002
2001
2000
1999
1998
1997
1996
1995
1994
1993
1992
1991
1990
1989
1988
1987
1986
1985
1984
1983
1982

FILM

# A.I. ARTIFICIAL INTELLIGENCE

CREDITS
DIRECTOR: **STEVEN SPIELBERG**
PRODUCTION DESIGNER: **RICK CARTER**
VISUAL EFFECTS SUPERVISORS: **SCOTT FARRAR, DENNIS MUREN**
BASED ON THE SHORT STORY: **"SUPERTOYS LAST ALL SUMMER LONG," BRIAN ALDISS**
SCREEN STORY: **IAN WATSON**
SCREENPLAY: **STEVEN SPIELBERG**
PRODUCERS: **STEVEN SPIELBERG, BONNIE CURTIS, KATHLEEN KENNEDY**
ORIGINAL CONCEPT DESIGNS: **CHRIS BAKER**

*A.I.* is a future fairy tale, a loose recreation of Pinocchio's adventures, set in 2051, which revolves around the deeper issue of sentience. This long-gestating Kubrick project was finally taken over by the master of modern fairy stories, Steven Spielberg, and makes up one of his most mature, intriguing, and spectacular works.

To a submerged and then frozen Manhattan by way of the pleasure pits and sensual delights of Rouge City and the mania of the Flesh Fair, A.I.'s science fantasy has an ethereal, intimate quality which makes it markedly different from the Sturm und Drang of that breed of sci-fi film which belongs to the digital effects actioner.

This is reflected in how Production Designer Rick Carter created the basis of his production design for the motion picture: "I always saw this as The Wizard of Oz. Everything I get to be involved in on this picture is like moving from one entire world to another. Each thing is in some ways almost entirely separate and different. Even contradictory."

This shifting from one world to another came from Kubrick's original conceptualizing of the piece. "One of the dramatic ideas Stanley Kubrick had told Steven that he wanted to explore in the structure of this film was what he called 'mode jerks.' These were abrupt changes and dramatic leaps from one distinct world to another. He had utilized this dramatic visual juxtaposition before in *2001*, especially in the cut between the bone flying up into the air and the spaceship. I'd never seen as many in one film, however, as there were in *A.I.*" [1]

>>>

"ONE OF THE DRAMATIC IDEAS STANLEY KUBRICK HAD TOLD STEVEN SPIELBERG THAT HE WANTED TO EXPLORE IN THE STRUCTURE OF THIS FILM WAS WHAT HE CALLED 'MODE JERKS.' THESE WERE ABRUPT CHANGES AND DRAMATIC LEAPS FROM ONE DISTINCT WORLD TO ANOTHER." RICK CARTER

IMAGES

01 Chris Baker created hundreds of illustrations in collaboration with Stanley Kubrick to develop locations.
02 Rouge City toll booths as they appear on screen.
03 Creating a set detail of the Pleasure City.
04 Dr. Know's set construction.

2004
2003
2002
**2001**
2000
1999
1998
1997
1996
1995
1994
1993
1992
1991
1990
1989
1988
1987
1986
1985
1984
1983
1982

01

02

03

04

05

06

07

*A.I.* was one of Kubrick's long-gestating projects that he had been particularly active in developing for three years in the early 1990s. Together with British artist Chris Baker, they created a detailed visual road map for the movie. This, along with a 100-page treatment, was eventually to be the basis for Spielberg's screenplay. Kubrick had been in long discussions with him over the picture, having come to an impasse on moving it foreword. On Kubrick's death, it was a natural process that the project should move on to Spielberg, who wanted to complete the project to honor their friendship, along with the fact that both Directors realized the movie was developing into territory—that of the adult fairy tale—that was more appropriate for Spielberg.

>>>

"YOU ARE LITERALLY THRUST INTO
ANOTHER REALM THAT IS SO DIFFERENT
AND ENTIRELY UNPREDICTABLE."
RICK CARTER

## IMAGES

01  *Rouge City*, an urban pleasure capital, as conceived in this production painting.
02-05  Fiberglass building scale models offer an exuberant appreciation of the female form.
06-07  Process shot layers used to make up final composites for the City.
08  Gigolo Joe and David in thrall to the hedonistic city..
04-06  Fiberglass building scale models offer an exuberant appreciation of the female form.
09-11  Stages of effects layers, from blue screen to final processed frame.

2004
2003
2002
**2001**
2000
1999
1998
1997
1996
1995
1994
1993
1992
1991
1990
1989
1988
1987
1986
1985
1984
1983
1982

01

12 ——— THE FLESH FAIR ——— Faygon 11/1/00

03

THIS NATURAL 'BOWL' OBVIOUSLY GIVES THE CROWD A GOOD VIEW OF THE
ACTION ABOUT TO TAKE PLACE AND AVOIDS THE USE OF SEATING.
TECHNICALLY IT ALSO PROVIDES QUITE A CONTROLLED LANDSCAPE TO WORK IN.

01

11 ——— THE FLESH FAIR Faygon 11/1/00

02
THIS PARKLAND WITH ITS SLOPING ARCHITECTURE CREATES AN IDEAL AMPHITHEATRE FOR
THE FAIR. THERE IS ALSO A SUGGESTION THAT IT IS QUITE CLOSE TO AREAS THAT ARE NOW
SWAMPLAND THUS THE 'LAW' IS NOT TOO CLOSE AT HAND!

IMAGES

01-02 The Flesh Fair concept drawings by Chris Baker.
03 Photograph of the Flesh Fair set.
04-06 Visualizations of Dr. Know's info booth: "Fast food
for thought, served up 24 hours a day."

04

06

05

The contradictory nature of *A.I.*'s environment is central to its appeal. Carter offers a breakdown: "Specifically, the movie was divided into three parts. The first section was a domestic drama, set in the future, sometime after the ice caps had melted and coastal cities—including New York City—had been submerged by the oceans. Because the movie was primarily a fairy tale, Steven and producer Kathy Kennedy decided not to show a lot of other forms of advanced technology in this part of the film. The main character, the ten-year-old robot David (played by Haley Joel Osment,) represented how far we had come." In this way, *A.I.* introduces us slowly to a world populated by artificially intelligent cyborgs, and cryogenic storage (the Swinton family who "adopt" David, the first robot programed to love, have a terminally ill child frozen while a cure can be found for the malady.)

The beginning of the film was almost entirely shot on soundstages in L.A. David is introduced into the Swinton's family. He attempts to integrate into the house—an interior which builds on Kubrick and Baker's rough designs by taking further design cues from Disneyland's 1960s House of Tomorrow, and architect Frank Lloyd Wright. "Responding to a suggestion by cinematographer Janusz Kaminski, we utilized vertical panes of textured glass as a cinematic device to not only divide rooms, but also as a way for the camera to be outside of the scenes and peer in. Our goal was to make this set—inspired by Photoshop set illustrations by James Clyne, and beautifully decorated by Nancy Haigh—appear inviting for David, but also just a bit cold and distant. After all, he would not actually be permitted to stay here for very long."

>>>

2004
2003
2002
**2001**
2000
1999
1998
1997
1996
1995
1994
1993
1992
1991
1990
1989
1988
1987
1986
1985
1984
1983
1982

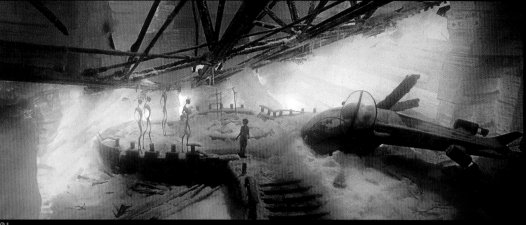

01

02

The second act turns into a "road movie," as David wanders through what the production dubbed the "Snow White Forest," and becomes embroiled in the Flesh Fair, where robots are slaughtered in the name of entertainment. Created as an amphitheater, an anarchic environment halfway between a rave and a Cirque du Soleil performance, the Flesh Fair is a stark example of the recurring circular motif that is echoed throughout the diverse milieux David travels through. It is used to interconnect the film's array of spaces and times, binding the robots' 2000-year journey together.

As David enters Rouge City in his search for the Blue Fairy, the film also moves into its most sensual phase. "The city had been originally designed by Chris to appear like Las Vegas gone sex crazy," states Carter. "We all loved his designs, especially the bridge entrance through the open mouths. So many of his drawings became the basis for the digital imagery."

Scott Farrar and Dennis Muren of I.L.M. supervised the creation of the cityscape. The environments combined blue screen live action footage with virtual environments, minatures and full-size set detailing, to present a convincing neon-colored, carnal-tinged metropolis. Rouge City is a maximilist paradise of sensational imagery. The X-rated curves of the architecture communicate a whimsical and unique vernacular that we haven't seen before—a futurescape that is neither overtly dystopic, Gothic or grimey, nor modernist and angular.

70S    AI — INTO THE ICE —

Fangona 26/7/95

03

15

— EXCAVATION SITE —

THE CRAFT FINALLY PEELS OFF REVEALING THE FERRIS WHEEL ....

04

The sterile interiors which begin the film give way to the degenerate Disneyland of Rouge City, filled with the hedonistic and salacious, leading to a rotten New York City, decayed, abandoned, and submerged. Finally, vast ice excavations invaded by floating "transhuman" architecture complete David's journey, from android to "real boy."

While a watery Manhattan sluices away the sleek extravagances of Rouge City, it is the far-flung future excavations, when David is reanimated, which cleanse the visual palette. The geometric abstractions of the "alien" architecture (actually post-human, post-android) offer a return to simplicity and serenity, and an opportunity to reflect on the film's rich architectural backdrops.

06

07

### IMAGES

01–02  The Excavation production painting and set: "This is where the movie takes its biggest jump of 2000 years," says Rick Carter.
03–04  The final form of the set was not dissimilar to Baker and Kubrick's sketches, and was followed closely in the storyboards.
05  The deep future denouement to *A.I.* where the transhumans excavate David's resting place.
06–07  David's quest to become a real boy is nearly complete when he discovers the Blue Fairy.

【 SOURCE 】

[1] ORIGINAL NOTES PROVIDED BY RICK CARTER (10/2004)

2004
2003
2002
2001
2000
1999
1998
1997
1996
1995
1994
1993
1992
1991
1990
1989
1988
1987
1986
1985
1984
1983
1982

**FILM**

# METROPOLIS

01

02

Legendary manga artist Osamu Tezuka, most famous for his Astro Boy character, is generally accepted to be the founding father of this wildly successful media in his native Japan. Tezuka's distinctive drawing style is brought to the screen in an adaptation by animé director Rintaro. Apparently inspired by the poster of the original sci-fi classic, Fritz Lang's *Metropolis* (1927), Tezuka's vision is reimagined by Rintaro and Katsuhiro Otomo (the director of legendary animation, *Akira* (1988), who adapted Tezuka's original story.

Rintaro and Otomo have altered Tezuka's original manga vision to their own ends. The sprawling metropolis of Tezuka's manga is altered in favor of a layered society—humans in gilded skyscrapers at the zenith, and robot workers in the lower zones, primarily existing in a vast, gloomy subterranean network.

This Jazz-era metropolis is layered as the archetypal future comic book city. Latticed girders and riveted ironwork hold up impressive towers. Moving walkways and hover cars float along elevated highways, transporting citizens. The candy colors give the film a hint of the theme park and fairground ride. Monorails and zeppelins wend through the city, in and out of the tunneled midriff of the city's skyscrapers. Art deco-inspired, computer-generated animé backgrounds are replete with expressionist-inspired, shaded 3D structures. This CG rendering is placed against traditional 2D, almost super-deformed, character animations in an odd but distinctive mix.

**CREDITS**

DIRECTOR: **RINTARO**

ART DIRECTOR: **SHUICHI HIRATA**

SCREENPLAY: **KATSUHIRO OTOMO**

ADAPTED FROM THE COMIC: **OSAMU TEZUKA**

PRODUCER: **YUTAKA MASEBA**

ANIMATED EFFECTS: **MAD HOUSE**

03

04

05

06

07

08

09

"It's sort of the visual style of the American 1930s, things like in the style of the buildings, like in the future," Rintaro summizes. "But there are zeppelins flying in the film. It's in a future setting, but I wanted to include something like a nostalgia for the American 1930s."

In its opening scene, straight promenades lined with modernist boxes of classic proportions render a fascimile of the clean lines of Albert Speer's architecture for Hitler. This slightly menacing evocation of fascistic constructions may be deliberate, as the overwhelming architectural image from the film is the huge Ziggurat. It dominates the skyline, rendered in striking CG. It is like an exaggerated Senate House, the University of London building that was earmarked as Hitler's Nazi Party headquarters if England had been conquered.

The Ziggurat hides a deadly laser that can be fired from its apex. Inside the tower, a complex series of cogs and gears are used to lower and raise the construction to the roof. The combination of these, along with the industrial nature of the lower zones, with their funiculars, large revolving turbines, pipes, and similar infrastructure, embellishes the movie with an innovative "steampunk meets art deco" appearance. *Metropolis* takes classic science fiction elements and turns them into the peculiar and original.

IMAGES

01 The Ziggurat is the architectural focal point of *Metropolis*.
02 Industrial-age detailing on the towers.
03–06 Street scene from *Metropolis* detailing the different stages of animation, compositing structural layers with traffic.
07 The steampunk esthetic embodied by the Ziggurat's laser.
08 Profile of the Ziggurat's unfolding laser.
09 Dramatic nighttime lighting transformation of the Ziggurat, evoking Jazz-era America.

2004
2003
2002
2001
2000
1999
1998
1997
1996
1995
1994
1993
1992
1991
1990
1989
1988
1987
1986
1985
1984
1983
1982

+ 3 RING CIRCUS, ASYLUM VISUAL EFFECTS, DIGITAL FIREPOWER, IMAGINARY FORCES, INDUSTRIAL LIGHT & MAGIC, KURTZ & FRIENDS ANIMATION, MILKSHAKE MEDIA, PDI/DREAMWORKS, PIXEL LIBERATION FRONT

**FILM**　　　　**VISUAL EFFECTS**

# MINORITY REPORT

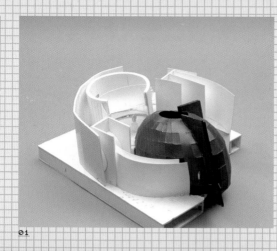

01

02

**CREDITS**

DIRECTOR: STEVEN SPIELBERG
PRODUCTION DESIGNER: ALEX MCDOWELL
SHORT STORY: PHILIP K. DICK
SCREENPLAY: SCOTT FRANK, JON COHEN
PRODUCERS: JAN DE BONT, BONNIE CURTIS, GERALD R. MOLEN,
WALTER F. PARKES, RONALD SHUSETT
VISUAL EFFECTS SUPERVISOR: SCOTT FARRAR

03

04

Philip K. Dick imagined a nameless, near-future U.S. city that is free of murderous crime. Precogs (Precognitives), three psychics who can see into the future, allow the Justice Department Precrime Unit to intercept and punish the guilty before the crime is committed. *Minority Report* offers a future where the environment is shaped by discreet technology. Arthur C. Clarke stated that: "Any sufficiently advanced technology is indistinguishable from magic." Spielberg conjures up a magical environment based on feasible science.

The visualization of *Minority Report*'s future came out of a think tank brought together by Production Designer Alex McDowell and Director Steven Spielberg. They effectively create an imagined future from the natural evolution of current technological advances: a future based on science fact rather than pure fiction.

IMAGES

01  Model of the Precrime H.Q. with tank at the center.
02  Precog's float in a tank of "photon milk."
03  *Minority Report*'s Precog set under construction.
04  Concept painting of the Precog set.

2004
2003
**2002**
2001
2000
1999
1998
1997
1996
1995
1994
1993
1992
1991
1990
1989
1988
1987
1986
1985
1984
1983
1982

01

02

03

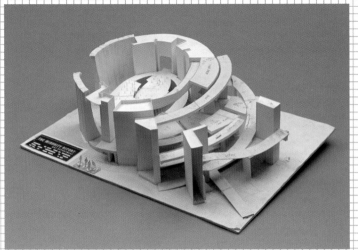

04

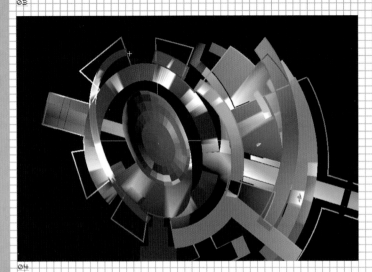

05

06

07

08

09

**IMAGES**

01 Precrime headquarters set being built.
02 Layers of transparency take shape on the set.
03 Early rendering of Precrime H.Q.
04–05 Early overhead 3D set render and scale model of the set.
06 Painting of Washington D.C.'s futuristic overspill, on the other side of the Potomac River to the City's historic center.
07 Mall environment concept.
08 Historic Washington D.C. is divided from new development.
09 Concept for *Minority Report's* futuristic tower blocks .

"The first meeting with Spielberg for *Minority Report* gave me enough information to run with for the next three months," states McDowell who, with a researcher, had prepared over 300 images to scan through and gather rapid feedback on to make the most of this preliminary dialog. "It's been my experience that the broad strokes of the direction of the entire film are laid out in this initial conversation. You've only just read the script and it's as fresh as it will ever be. The Director has been mulling it over for months and is ready to download all his thoughts."

Spielberg wanted the movie's tone to be such that the audience on initial viewing would be split as to whether precrime was a good thing, or a horrific loss of civil liberties. "As a framework for this McGuffin, he wanted the setting of the story to be an apparently benign, non-apocalyptic future, where society, technology, and urban life have set up a successful balance. The wide framing of this was in the ecologically green layering of the city, where vehicles run on green fuel, and society is long-lived and healthy. This is a society that has achieved the promise that we recognize in modern technology, but that has not yet been achieved." [1]

As an antithesis to the sci-fi fable, *A.I.* (see page 78), Spielberg constantly pulled everyone back from fictional excesses—or the more outlandish probabilities—to make the story and its environment more plausible, accessible for a wide audience: "It was important to Spielberg that the film was not considered science fiction, but Future Reality, a description we coined... He wanted to keep the audience grounded, with the idea that the story of precrime would lose all its impact if the audience could say 'Oh, that would never happen.'"

*Minority Report* creates a subtle but immensely rich world with an array of ideas embedded within the surroundings that reward repeated viewing. The stated aim was to produce the "ultimate wirelessly networked, ubiquitously connected urban environment." Due to a number of rare circumstances which arose during production, McDowell was able to fashion a highly cinematic and dense information environment based on bleeding-edge research. "*Minority Report* was an eye-opening example of how much the preproduction research period can feed the fabric of a film," explains McDowell.

>>>

2004
2003
**2002**
2001
2000
1999
1998
1997
1996
1995
1994
1993
1992
1991
1990
1989
1988
1987
1986
1985
1984
1983
1982

01

02

"After a couple of months of initial research, the producers set up a think tank for Steven and his team to meet a group of futurist scientists, sociologists, and suchlike. This was an interesting process. We were given a long list of recommended specialists to choose from or suggest, and from the condensed list came a group of a dozen leaders in their respective field who spent two days in a Santa Monica hotel in a large group discussion. Out of that back and forth—us bringing our narrative-driven, film-based ideas to the table, they brainstorming science, technology, and social solutions within the parameters of our brief—came the groundwork for the design of the film, and also for some crucial script ideas. Scott Frank and I continued this interchange as we developed our respective work, so that the design and writing were far more integrated than they would have been with a preexisting script."

The "deep access" elicited by the Spielberg name gave the idea of the think tank momentum: "Initially, the think tank was very important, and useful. But as much for what we disagreed with as the inspiration it provided. For example, the sociologists pretty much unanimously disagreed with our pre-existing approach to develop the city of Washington D.C. vertically. They were insistent that the future would be a New Urbanist utopia of low-level suburbia." The filmmakers dropped this idea, deciding that a setting akin to Disney's manufactured "perfect town" of Celebration, Florida, would not be as exhilarating as the sleek vertiginous district they were envisioning. McDowell puts it succinctly: "A car chase through endless suburbs would have been less cinematic than the vertical Maglev chase, and the horizontal spread of suburbs would not have encapsulated our symbolic, if simplistic, layered society.

"Other ideas these sessions brought forth that had intriguing implications for a future world included bio-engineered hybrid pets, and bio-architecture with rooms that would change their form to suit the occupant. Ultimately though, they did not serve Spielberg's sense of a future environment an audience could immediately associate with.

"From these initial meetings, we were able to have well-informed discussions with a bunch of corporations who in turn gave us access to their futurists and developers. We were also invited to visit M.I.T.'s MediaLab where our guide turned out to be John Underkoffler, a brilliant scientist who eventually came on board the film as our in-house science advisor.

Writer Scott Frank was hired to write a new script at the same time, giving the Production Designer the opportunity to shape the environments the script would explore, and play out in. "Because there was no working script in place when I was first hired, we made the decision to first investigate a broad overview of a world that could contain all aspects of the narrative, and then to extract from that overview the specific details of the world that the script could pursue to create the customary and more narrow visual 'corridor' that would frame the final script," says McDowell. Involving the Production Designer from a pre-script stage is still relatively unusual, but since this film's production is becoming increasingly commonplace, as digital effects and environments need to be factored into the script's milieu.

IMAGES

01 Production illustration contrasting new and old Washington D.C.
02 Rendering of street level area, where the production cues for this strata are grimier than the gleaming city heights.
03–04 The Maglev highway flows up and over city structures.
05 Exploring the dramatic camera angles for the stunning set piece Maglev chase.
06 Production drawing as a basis for creating previz work.
07 Production picture of transport system flowing over buildings.

92

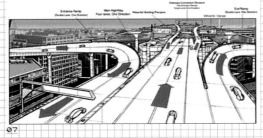

This echoed Spielberg's wish to explore the implications of intelligent environments: "The most striking thing for me was that George Orwell's prophecy really comes true, not in the twentieth century, but in the twenty-first century. What little privacy we have now will be completely evaporated in 20 to 30 years, as we'll be able to see through walls and rooftops."[2]

This depth of research resulted in McDowell creating an ever-evolving document he christened the "2050 Bible." It became the central source of knowledge for key members of the crew as they came on-stream during production. It also became the driving force, according to McDowell, for him to create a fully digital art department, using a networked database to use the production's digital resources efficiently.

Spielberg shelved *Minority Report* temporarily eight months into pre-production in order to fasttrack the filming of *A.I.* (see page 78), a film passed on to him to direct due to the demise of Stanley Kubrick. A year later, design recommenced, enabling the design department the luxury of drilling down on the wide view of the future world already established. Design elements that are usually passed over due to lack of time were honed for the next 10 months in service to the more specific arc of the story. "Normally, you design a film, wait a year for its release and then bemoan the many irreversible mistakes you have made." In contrast, the extended but unusual circumstances of production presented McDowell "the perfect way to approach a film of this kind."

The geographic basis of *Minority Report* developed from the previously mentioned realworld restrictions of Capitol Hill and its surrounds. The production needed a tall city for visual and symbolic impact. "That set in motion the thought that a giant city would spring up in Virginia, directly adjacent to D.C. but across the Potomac River and outside the zoning laws." An intricate backstory supported the development of this metropolis. They created the need for the authorities to cluster the public into a 50-mile radius of the precog effect so Precrime policing could be effective. This social engineering gave a compelling reason for a dense urban landscape, with the buildings in this area rising dramatically to maintain the population within these limits.

>>>

"These scientists and thinkers were as interested in getting involved in a film project like *Minority Report* as we were in tapping into their knowledge, and the ongoing dialog allowed us to create a connective logic for the film that helps the audience to become immersed."

Other ideas, such as the actual zoning regulations in Washington D.C., ideas about technology, narrowcast advertising, and the interactive intelligence of future devices, were all applied to create a believable atmosphere. Indeed, the interactive marketing activated through retinal scanning John Anderton activates in a chase scene elevates what could have been a stock scene into a highly memorable one—*Minority Report*'s utopian environment suddenly becomes another pursuer. In an instant the setting is transformed into a claustrophobic nightmare the protagonist is unable to escape.

2004
2003
**2002**
2001
2000
1999
1998
1997
1996
1995
1994
1993
1992
1991
1990
1989
1988
1987
1986
1985
1984
1983
1982

Ø1

Ø2

Ø3

"As these buildings grow, vertically and horizontally—we imagined a horizontal development in the upper levels that would incorporate public transportation, Maglev roadways, pedestrian thoroughfares, greened recreation areas, and giant malls, hence the Mall City setting—they overshadowed older development below, reducing property values and creating an impoverished and under-serviced Slum City. This logic allowed for the Maglev chase and gave Anderton a way to escape the all-seeing consumer targeting networked with police surveillance. D.C. remains as the old money seat of power, unchanged despite the futuristic setting. It was a basic decision to allow older architecture to remain in the film—after all we live and work now in buildings that might be many decades, if not centuries, old.

"The silhouette of the city remained familiar if tall, with the only radical new architecture being the Maglev transportation system that adds a ribbon development both vertically and horizontally. We also added a large amount of green space, figuring that the zoning of Mall City would demand a plateau of recreation areas proportional to the vertical construction."

They looked at a number of influential contemporary architecture practices to frame the construction of this urban utopia: Ken Yeang, Ushida-Findley, and Nicholas Grimshaw. McDowell also met with a plethora of progressive architects, including Greg Lynn of FORM and Frank Gehry's office.

"Jean Nouvel was the primary influence on the Precrime set, and Takasaki Masaharu's Kihoku Astronomical Museum on the Precog Chamber. Cesar Pelli's Petrona Towers, Hiroshi Hara's Shin-Umeda City Development, Arata Isozaki's work in the 1960s, and Dutch architects M.V.D.V.R., who were influential in the idea of a horizontal Mall City development. Paul Rudolph's work was the basis of Anderton's Apartment and the skyscraper the Maglev chase is based around."

Inspiration was not however confined to architects. "I was also influenced by fashion designers such as Issey Miyake. The surfacing of the Precog chamber was inspired by Issey Miyake's pleated fabrics. Also Rei Kawakubo, and Hussein Chalayan, whose work is architectonic and sculptural, and concentrates on structure rather than surface." The interior settings further showcase new facets of this society, enhancing the film's credibility.

The Precrime set was particularly beguiling for cinematographer Janusz Kaminski: "These sets are beautiful. Very contemporary, very sensual. With curves and straight lines, lots of glass and metallic surfaces. I like it when the material used in the set design has a metallic surface because subsequently the light is reflected beautifully. If the set has glass, you get reflection and you can also see through the glass, so you get layering. That is what the world of *Minority Report* happens to be. It is very densely layered."[3]

"It is often true that a script does not offer much description for the Designer," elucidates McDowell. "Or if it does, it is often superseded by the global design of the film, which might suggest a different approach to a specific scene. In *Minority Report*, the Precogs are described in the short story (our starting point) and original script as more outwardly monstrous victims in vertical isolation tanks, separate from one another. Spielberg's approach was far more subtle and apparently benign; that the Precogs become an iconic and peaceful image, and that their suffering is more slowly revealed."

The design department used extensive previs throughout pre-production and production to create live-action sets, and as 3D and prop data for V.F.X. and animation. "Its value to the design process is very wide. We used it to design the Spyder sequence in the decaying hotel by building a virtual Technocrane in the virtual set and having the complex single-take camera move to determine the outline of the set, with no CG element except the Spyders themselves." These Spyders are advanced seekers the Precrime Unit uses to track down suspects. "We used it for the Hall of Containment set, which was almost all CG animation and was designed entirely in previs."

IMAGES

Ø1  The subterranean tenement set.
Ø2  Production painting showing tenement set overhead perspective.
Ø3  Overhead photo of the tenement set. Complex overhead camera movements through the apartment echo this angle.
Ø4  Production painting for the Hall of Containment, an update of Jeremy Bentham's classic Panopticon surveillance design.
Ø5  Carrying through vertical motifs at Precrime H.Q.

04

McDowell's team used Maya software to model sets, and details were often built using computer-controlled technology, to cut CNC foam panels, for example. Accurate scale models of such things as vehicle designer Harald Belker's Maglev cars were 3D "printed" using rapid prototyping equipment. McDowell's work illustrates how production design has had to adapt. "With access to this whole new level of digital tools, the role of Production Designer is becoming increasingly important, at the core of a flow of data that is going to every creative department."

Ironically, McDowell's development of the production design department during the production echoes *Minority Report*'s own examination of data flow, the implications of pervasive information networks, and a future of intelligent agents and predictive technologies. Ultimately, Spielberg's future reality is a highly prescient and relevant film in a contemporary world of data-mining, satellite monitoring, and "preemptive strikes."

05

Much of the credit for this film's significance, its exceptionally convincing illusion of believability, must go to McDowell. "Production design is reading a story, a script, and holding the vision and atmosphere of those words in your mind long enough to try to create a pure representation—of a space that exists in two and three dimensions, at the same time, in time... the emotional and the physical wrapped into space that is both abstract and symbolic, historical and representational. The characters and the dialog affect the space, and the written description affects the space, but it is the combination that makes the space."

[ SOURCES ]

[1] ALEX MCDOWELL, ORIGINAL INTERVIEW, MATT HANSON (10/2004)

[2] *Minority Report Special Edition* DVD COMMENTARY

[3] IBID

2004
2003
2002
2001
2000
1999
1998
1997
1996
1995
1994
1993
1992
1991
1990
1989
1988
1987
1986
1985
1984
1983
1982

**+** CINESITE, RHYTHM & HUES, IMAGE SAVANT
USING PIXAR'S SLIM, RENDERMAN, CINEON,
PHOTOSHOP, DEEP PAINT, STUDIO PAINT, MAYA,
SPORE & PROPRIETARY TOOLS.

**FILM**

**VISUAL EFFECTS**

# SOLARIS

Ø1

**CREDITS**
DIRECTOR: **STEVEN SODERBERGH**
PRODUCTION DESIGNER: **PHILIP MESSINA**
SCREENPLAY: **STEVEN SODERBERGH**
ADAPTED FROM THE NOVEL BY: **STANISLAW LEM**
PRODUCERS: **JAMES CAMERON, JON LANDAU, RAE SANCHINI**

02

03

The 1972 original of *Solaris*—the Soviet equivalent of Kubrick's *2001*—by Russian director Andrei Tarkovsky, is one of the great science fiction films, so it takes some audacity to remake it. Steven Soderbergh brings this cerebral sci-fi into the new millennium with panache, his trademark visual sheen, and editing that seamlessly gels with the dislocation of the film.

"I'm not interested in making a film about what technology is going to be like a few decades from now," Soderbergh stressed about the project. His motivation was more to create an off-world experience designed to give the viewer an off-kilter experience to parallel protaganist Dr Chris Kelvin's. Kelvin is asked to investigate the space station Prometheus—an orbiting science expedition around the mysterious planetary body of Solaris—which has seen its scientists exhibiting increasingly strange behavior. Once aboard the orbiting station, he is confronted by suicide and the image of his dead wife. His memories literally come back to haunt him.

The production designer, and long-time Soderbergh collaborator Philip Messina, had to convey the isolation, sensory deprivation, and strange psychic environment of *Solaris*. Messina's approach was that: "Solaris needed to feel real because it is a love story, not a hardware film. Outer space is simply the backdrop." To illicit this sense of realism, Soderbergh and Messina decided to develop the interior and exterior forms of Prometheus based on the International Space Station, devising a more industrial, hi-tech, steel and composites look, compared to the Mosfilm original. Messina's reasoning: "What we liked about the International Space Station were the textures and the fact that not everything had been figured out yet. There are odd pieces that stick off the walls."

The emotional intensity and oppressive ambience of the movie was emphasized by Messina's creation of claustrophobic, true-to-life interiors that conserved space just like the real thing. The lack of portals and limited headroom strengthens this sense of entrapment. The set was a two-story construction measuring 150 by 220 feet. Exteriors were all done using CG.

>>>

IMAGES

01 Steely blues and grays permeate outer space *Solaris*.
02 Concept painting of Prometheus overlooking the Planet Solaris.
03 The surface of Solaris had a number of distinct looks developed for it, created using the custom software Spore by Image Savant.

2004
2003
2002
**2001**
2000
1999
1998
1997
1996
1995
1994
1993
1992
1991
1990
1989
1988
1987
1986
1985
1984
1983
1982

Ø1

Ø2

Ø3

Ø4

IMAGES

Ø1 The film's final space architecture lies somewhere between the look of the original *Solaris* and real-life space capsules.
Ø2–Ø3 Actual space capsule interiors were refined through concept drawings.
Ø4–Ø5 The delicate space structures of *Solaris* are worlds away from space fantasy craft.
Ø6 Concept painting of the *2001: A Space Odyssey*, Soderbergh's reference for "authentic" cinematic space travel.
Ø7–Ø8 Director Steven Soderbergh wanted to keep the film as far within the framework of reality as possible. So the space technology and craft were extrapolated from current designs, most notably the International Space Station.

Cinesite created 3D models of the Prometheus and Athena spacecrafts. "We didn't model every single piece of the spacecraft. Instead, we used textures for a lot of that sort of detail," says Cinesite's John Hewitt, who supervised the sequences featuring the vessels. "The textures were very important for adding realism to the spacecraft. Because these ships move slowly and are seen at 4K resolution, they had to be extremely detailed." [1]

*2001* (1968) was a benchmark for creating the models. Because they needed to generate a heightened sense of realism through the animations, textures were applied to surfaces to give the illusion of detailing using Studio Paint, Photoshop, and Deep Paint. Hewitt adds: "Soderbergh was inspired by *2001: A Space Odyssey*, and in that film the spaceship was white. Initially, we started with textures that were much more metallic and darker. But he kept asking us to clean them up and go with whiter materials. When we did that, though, it got more and more difficult to see the textures."

Tom Smith, the Visual Effects Supervisor at Cinesite elaborates on the complex opening sequence: "[Kelvin] is traveling in a ship which has a small pod that detaches and takes him to dock with Prometheus. We come very close to this docking bay, which fills the whole screen—and it's all CG. Because the ships are constantly moving, all the bits and pieces on their surfaces cast shadows that are always changing. The amount of detail that you see when you get up close is where the payoff is."[2]

To make sure they had this detail, they used processor-intensive ray-tracing techniques to heighten the reflective surfaces of the craft. This also neatly intersected with Soderbergh and Messina's use of in-camera reflections, glimmering surfaces, flashes, and flares, to evoke a future space between memory and reality. "We wanted the colors of the Prometheus to be soothing in both a realistic and dreamlike way," explains Messina. "We used a lot of color, but all within the blues and greens—and even they are grayed out except for the Cold Room, the station's computer center, which we gave more intense blue color. Wherever I used blues, I also added some gray. I wanted the background to have a more homogeneous feeling, so the characters would stand out. There are a lot of textures, but what you see is light and shadow and not lots of colors." It is in this way *Solaris* induces a subtle future reality from contemporary environments both on- and off-world.

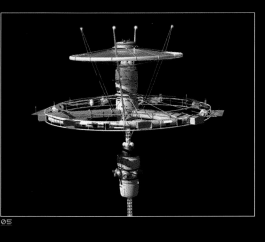

05

06

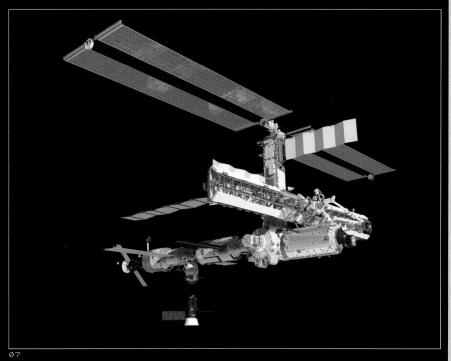

07

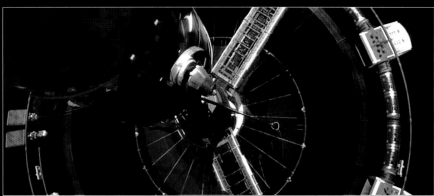

08

【 SOURCES 】

[1] "WORLD OF EMOTION,"
*Computer Graphics World*, AUDREY DOYLE (12/2002)

[2] "SODERBERGH'S HIGH-RES SPACE ODYSSEY,"
*Millimeter*, ELLEN WOLFF (11/2002)

2004
2003
2002
2001
2000
1999
1998
1997
1996
1995
1994
1993
1992
1991
1990
1989
1988
1987
1986
1985
1984
1983
1982

**FILM**

**VISUAL EFFECTS**

# CODE 46

+ **SMOKE AND MIRRORS**

Ø1

The world of *Code 46* is one where global warming and concurrent climate changes have seen the rest of the world become overrun with desert. There is "al fuera," the world outside, and inside, gleaming, luminous city states—affluent urban environments that have retrenched behind protected zones. Like Jean-Luc Godard's *Alphaville* (1965), it creates a convincing alternate near-future urban reality from "found" locations—in this case, Shanghai, Dubai, and Jaipur—all jigsawed together to create the megalopolis of the future. It deliberately eschews the artifice of imagined worlds, an antidote to an overload of CG-enhanced sci-fi realities.

Ø2

**CREDITS**
DIRECTOR: **MICHAEL WINTERBOTTOM**
PRODUCTION DESIGNER: **MARK TILDESLEY**
SCREENPLAY: **FRANK COTTRELL BOYCE**
PRODUCER: **ANDREW EATON**

03

04

*Code 46's* future was formed from prolific British director Michael Winterbottom's experiences of cross-border migration—the road blocks and bureaucracy—while filming his previous film *In this World* (2002), which followed the journey of a couple of Afghani refugees from Northern Pakistan to London. Thus, the idea of "papelles"—IDs as half-passport, half-visa—the documents needed to travel and gain access to the sheltered urban oases in this near-future came about.

Everything else is an extrapolation of the present, according to Winterbottom: "We said, Let's imagine that climate change means that areas that were once fertile are now desert, so the area around Shanghai is a desert. Let's imagine that the ozone layer is depleted and people are afraid to go out in the daytime, so they work at night. Also, let's imagine that because of these changes, living outside of a controlled urban environment is very hard, so everyone wants to live inside the city. Which means that the cities are even more densely populated than now, and in order to control that urban space, you have to have some kind of privatized visa system, which gives permission for some people to live in the city. But only those who have the official papelles... Meanwhile, the disenfranchised people who have no papelles live in the desert area, al fuera, beyond the city limits."

>>>

## IMAGES

01 Careful framing and choice of locations emphasize the "futuristic" nature of contemporary spaces.
02 *Code 46* is a polyglot world where Asian, and particularly Chinese influences are more evident.
03 Shanghai's waterfront, dominated by the Oriental Pearl Tower, acts as the most impressive *Code 46* set.
04 The sterile, neutral zones of Airport terminals contrast with the wild, earthy nature of "al fuera."

"WE DECIDED THAT IT WAS MORE IMPORTANT TO DEVELOP A CONSISTENT EMOTIONAL SPACE THAN TO CREATE A GADGET-RIDDEN FUTURISTIC WORLD."
MARK TILDESLEY

2004
**2003**
2002
2001
2000
1999
1998
1997
1996
1995
1994
1993
1992
1991
1990
1989
1988
1987
1986
1985
1984
1983
1982

Ø1

Ø2

Production Designer Mark Tildesley pieced together a "creative geography" for the film. A scene might be made up of a few different locations, different pieces of buildings existing in reality thousands of miles from each other. Tildesley thought, "The most interesting thing to do would be to try to fool the audience by taking the most interesting bits from each location. So you'd have the impression that you were walking out of a door in one city, but you'd actually end up walking out of it into completely different place, somewhere else entirely." They chose Shanghai and Dubai as locations because they have: "This extraordinary, contradictory architecture. In Shanghai there is Third World poverty in the shadow of some of the most modern skyscrapers in the world. In Dubai there is the skyscraper area of the city and then just behind it is the desert. It was those curious juxtapositions which were interesting and attractive."

The concept of the film was to foreground the love story with a genetic slant, so as not to bring too much attention to a futuristic world. Essentially, all the innovations that have happened are a less visible aspect of this reality. Tildesley explains: "We decided that it was more important to develop a consistent emotional space than a gadget-ridden futuristic world."

The space created by *Code 46* is a compelling, almost meditative, melancholic vision, muted and disquieting. The dream of globalization has soured into an overly surveilled and controlling world (echoes of the U.S. Patriot Act, here), where even sexual partners need to be DNA-vetted (a consequence of much of the population being born from in-vitro fertilization and originating from human clones). The film's East-meets-West outlook evokes the futurist visions of J.G. Ballard, where the vermilion sands of Third World deserts are interrupted only by run-down settlements and sleek shimmering citystate protectorates. Shanghai is a perfect location, as, more than any other city, it is currently undergoing a rapid transformation into "the city of the future." The already sci-fi-inflected design of the Oriental Pearl TV tower in Pudong clashes up against the art deco mansions of Shanghai's faded colonial past. Yet it makes perfect sense that Pudong's new skyscraper district should coexist with the older part of town, Puxi, across the Huangpu river.

*Code 46's* dystopic sci-fi reality is a world on the brink of destruction, fractured into citystates, internationalist but isolated. A world of transience, of airport check-ins, and motorway check points. Where people are as disconnected as the locations themselves. The glowing circular atrium of Shanghai's Grand Hyatt, located in the feng shui'd Jiang Mao tower, or the City's elevated highways, spiral people into themselves, into a reverie.

IMAGES

Ø1–Ø2 *Code 46* utilizes the sterile, high international architectural style of skyscrapers in Shanghai and Dubai, and contrasts them with Colonial pasts, echoing the film's protagonists' wish to dirty their genetic purity.
Ø3 The Jiang Mao Tower is China's ultimate embellished spin on skyscraper fashion.

03

2004
2003
2002
2001
2000
1999
1998
1997
1996
1995
1994
1993
1992
1991
1990
1989
1988
1987
1986
1985
1984
1983
1982

**FILM**

VISUAL EFFECTS

# THE MATRIX REVOLUTIONS

ESC, TIPPETT STUDIO, BUF COMPAGNIE, GIANT KILLER ROBOTS, SONY PICTURES IMAGEWORKS

Ø1

Ø2

Ø3

**CREDITS**
DIRECTORS: **ANDY & LARRY WACHOWSKI**
PRODUCTION DESIGNER: **OWEN PATERSON**
SCREENPLAY: **ANDY & LARRY WACHOWSKI**
PRODUCERS: **ANDREW MASON, ALEX PROYAS**
VISUAL EFFECTS SUPERVISOR: **JOHN GAETA, KIM LIBRERI, CRAIG HAYES (FOR TIPPETT)**

IMAGES

01, 03 Craig Hayes on Machine
City: "Things had to work in a normal
lighting environment and also in
'Neo-vision'—like an x-ray of the
energy, a nervous system. Inside
structures had to be built into all
the modeling."
02 Inside *The Matrix Reloaded*, the
absolute embodiment of a modern
Downtown of Corporate headquarters
and clusters of glass-fronted towers.

The Wachowski Brothers' *Matrix* trilogy stands
as a landmark in a genre that trades on the
spectacular. A deeply textured trilogy that gets
darker and more outlandish as it reaches its
climax, the Wachowskis' aim was to make a
live-action world straight off a graphic novel
page—a Japanese animé come to life. The
trilogy comprises an unprecedented number
of visual effects set pieces, and a grandiose
production design that takes in a subtly different
virtual present (the eponymous *Matrix* of the
title, designed by the machines to keep humans
in check), and a razed apocalyptic future world
(where humans are farmed for their energy by
machines).

In the finale to the trilogy, we get to experience
more of the architecture created by the
intelligent machines which now run the world.
"These films have two realities: the Matrix and
the real world," explains John Gaeta, who
oversaw the epic visual effects in the films.
"Now, we have a lot of environments in the 'real
world.' We have Zion, the tunnel systems that go
up to the surface of the Earth, and on the
surface, which the machine species has
populated. That is what Geof Darrow's strongest
imagery is based on. *Reloaded* focuses on
understanding the architecture of the *Matrix* and
the power structures within it. *Revolutions* spills
way out and takes us deep into the real world, as
far-reaching as the machines themselves, to the
source of the imprisonment of human beings
and the programs that run the *Matrix*. There are
layers and layers." [1]

>>>

2004
**2003**
2002
2001
2000
1999
1998
1997
1996
1995
1994
1993
1992
1991
1990
1989
1988
1987
1986
1985
1984
1983
1982

01

02

03

The concept designs that Darrow and the Wachowski Brothers devised were the driver for the final forms of machine architecture and set design. Making these designs reality fell to Production Designer, Owen Paterson, Gaeta's E.S.C. Entertainment, and Tippett Studio's team, overseen by Craig Hayes, among others.

Paterson states: "The films had a very descriptive script. The original *Matrix* set up this idea of the real world and the Matrix, essentially an illusion. When I came onto the production the real world was already conceptualized. Larry and Andy had done a lot of work with Darrow, the Conceptual Designer, to a point where the vision was very clear. What was left for me was to look at the line drawings and fill them in. They loved his concept of detail and the nuts-and-bolts look of the world. It was a very mechanical world, in real opposition to the organic nature of things. They were keen to achieve the next generation on from what mankind had built. Everything was to have the sense of conveying the silicon chip." [2]

The key part of the process that made everything gain momentum in the design was also the simplest to put into action. Paterson continues: "Along with Bill Pope, we figured out a visual key for the film, which is not so obvious in the first film but was a very decisive move. We decided the real world, outside the Matrix, would be cold, mechanic. So we would have a blue-gray color sense to the real world. Within the Matrix, it was natural to have a green hue, because we just thought of the basic computer monitor color, that of the green type on the black screen of early DOS-operating computers. It might appear strange now, but when you first read that script, it was not always clear which world you were in. It was easy to get lost, so coming up with those visual keys was really needed. I think it is something Ridley Scott does really well all the time, coming up with design decisions which may not appear obvious at the time. They are instinctive. The colors, in hindsight, were an obvious choice to implement, but they weren't at the time. The sequels really took the benefit of the milieu created by the first film."

IMAGES

01–02_ The Harvester fields, with vertical human farms in the distance, in the "real world" and in "Neo-vision."
03_ Tippett Studio used fractals and organic cues to add interest to the cold, hard-edged nature of a machine-dominated planet.
04–05_ The snaking tunnel system and Zion's underground docking bay involved complex CG modeling.

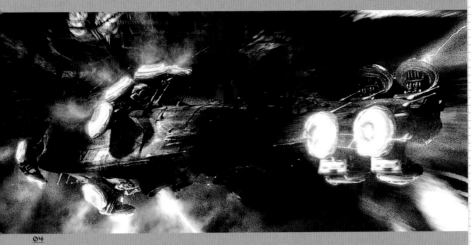

04

05

"WE DECIDED THE REAL WORLD, OUTSIDE THE MATRIX, WOULD BE COLD, MECHANIC... SO WE WOULD HAVE A BLUE-GRAY COLOR SENSE. WITHIN THE MATRIX, IT WAS NATURAL TO HAVE A GREEN HUE... THAT OF THE GREEN TYPE ON THE BLACK SCREEN OF EARLY DOS-OPERATING COMPUTERS." OWEN PATERSON

The sequels also upped the ante in creating landmark environments, such as the massive Machine City, derived from the machines' first city republic, Zero-One (additional background to the formation of the machine republic and the initial conflict between man and intelligent machine is neatly expanded upon in *The Animatrix* [2003] animé accompaniments to the trilogy.) Fox Stage 1 was utilized throughout production, which, at 400 feet long, is the largest stage in Australia. On it they created what Paterson calls his set "footprints," which ground the actors in a range of environments such as the penultimate, rain-drenched, Agent Smith-lined, City street, where Smith and Neo battle, and the walkways of the Zion docking station.

"In *Matrix* 2 and 3, Larry and Andy decided we would do one year of pre-production, one year of shooting, and one year of post-production. I obviously deferred to them on the set-up, and it basically meant I spent eight to 12 months working with Conceptual Artists and designing all the aspects of the film with the directors. They have a particularly clear concept of what they want visually as Directors. So my role becomes one of helping them flush out these environments. In the process, I am figuring out how to achieve these, and in pre-production lay down way before production everything to do with the look of the film. This intense preplanning had a benefit in that we could argue with the studio that we needed money to make a particular shot, and the associated set with it, many days before we were to actually do it. We needed to do this as we shot the sequels in 272 days, with a prior 65 days in the U.S. This was spread over three sets in the U.S., and over the 146 built in Australia.

"Once we had such a clear idea of the whole visual imagery for the film, it became an exercise in how to achieve it. How we could make happen what the Directors wanted. It was a flushing out process with them and an explanation of execution as opposed to an exploration of how it could physically look."

>>>

2004
2003
2002
2001
2000
1999
1998
1997
1996
1995
1994
1993
1992
1991
1990
1989
1988
1987
1986
1985
1984
1983
1982

Ø1

Although the film relies heavily on virtual environments, Paterson points out that most of the shots are based on real photos, and not on painted elements. One of the areas that had to be created truly digitally was the mammoth, 100-mile-wide Machine City Neo must reach to confront the Machine Godhead. The sequences involving this sprawling machine architecture, and the race through the Harvester Fields, were the domain of Tippett Studio. Craig Hayes' primary brief was to create something unique, and not simply a recreation of a "real city." They spent a lot of time thinking about how the architectural forms could be different, as the machines had no human constraints to narrow the form of these structures. Their ingenious solution was to use a procedurally driven approach. They created particle generation routines using Renderman, and further dynamics in Maya, then tweaked the results depending on what was created. In this way, they actually grew the City.

Hayes explains, "Initially, we had the key art from George Hall, who worked on color interpretations of the world, and Geof Darrow's conceptual illustrations. We had vistas to work with, but needed to engineer three dimensions and depth. So we thought about having key buildings and Hero Towers. There was a massive amount of information generated by the software routines we put in place, so we wanted to break it down. We defined tubes and connectors, and found real city analogies. So the program would grow suburbs and skyscrapers. We looked at other categories like water mains, and the infrastructure of the city, and made components for all of these things." [3]

Ø2

Ø2

IMAGES

Ø1–Ø3 Production paintings emphasize the zoomorphic nature of the Machine's structural forms.
Ø4–Ø8 Tippett Studio used particle systems and procedural routines to grow the miles of Machine City.
Ø9 "Darrow Towers" emphasize Crustacean elements.

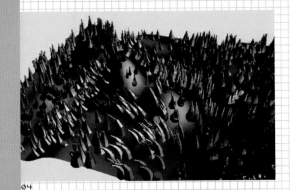

04

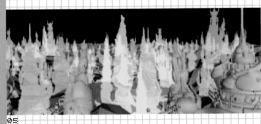

05

06

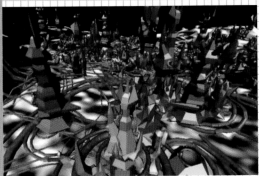

07

08

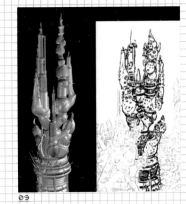

03

The software could only take it so far though until human operators took over to assess the best camera angles and manually add structures for dramatic interest. Some of the buildings generated were miles tall, which worked with the internal physics generated, but they drew this back so they were around 2,500 feet tall to make them more "believable." Hayes continues: "With the Hero Towers, we broke them down into stylistic components. For example, what we called the "Darrow Towers," which came from the engine, had a lobster-like top. Everything was modular so it became easier to create.

"In parallel, we had a team defining processes and visualizations. The job created multiple challenges. Things had to work in a normal lighting environment and also in 'Neo-vision.' This Neo-vision, like an x-ray of the energy—a nervous system—inside structures, had to be built into all the modeling.

We used Renderman so we could prepackage the geometries. It allowed us to define three to four different resolutions of buildings, stepping up from four polygons for those in the distance to so many polygons in a wireframe render you couldn't see through it. It also built in skeletons for the internal 'Neo-vision' structures."

Neo-vision is put to use most spectacularly when Neo comes face to face with the Machine's Godhead, where swarms of machine insects form a childlike "Buddha" face. The machine structures are exposed as alive with energy, a searing counterpoint to the gloom and magma-colors of a world under chemical clouds.

The scorched earth of the "real world" brings to mind the hellish landscape of *Blade Runner* (see page 18). Inside the Matrix, more film noir influences can be seen, similar in feel to the earlier *Dark City* (see page 68, also filmed in Australia. In fact, *The Matrix* used some set elements, such as the rooftop sets, created for *Dark City*.) But it is the evocation of a mecha-dominated universe, blending the best of Western and Asian sci-fi, that will be the trilogy's most lasting influence.

[ SOURCES ]

[1] "EXTRA MOMENTS," *Wired* INTERVIEW WITH JOHN GAETA, STEVE SILBERMAN, WWW.THELASTFREECITY.COM, (04/2003)

[2] OWEN PATERSON, ORIGINAL INTERVIEW, MATT HANSON (09/2004)

[3] CRAIG HAYES, ORIGINAL INTERVIEW, MATT HANSON (10/2004)

[4] "MAKING THE MATRIX," BARBARA ROBERTSON, *Computer Graphics World* (12/2003)

2003

2002
2001
2000
1999
1998
1997
1996
1995
1994
1993
1992
1991
1990
1989
1988
1987
1986
1985
1984
1983
1982

**FILM**

**VISUAL EFFECTS**

# WONDERFUL DAYS

\+

SOFTWARE: LIGHTWAVE,
3D STUDIO MAX,
AFTER EFFECTS, INFERNO

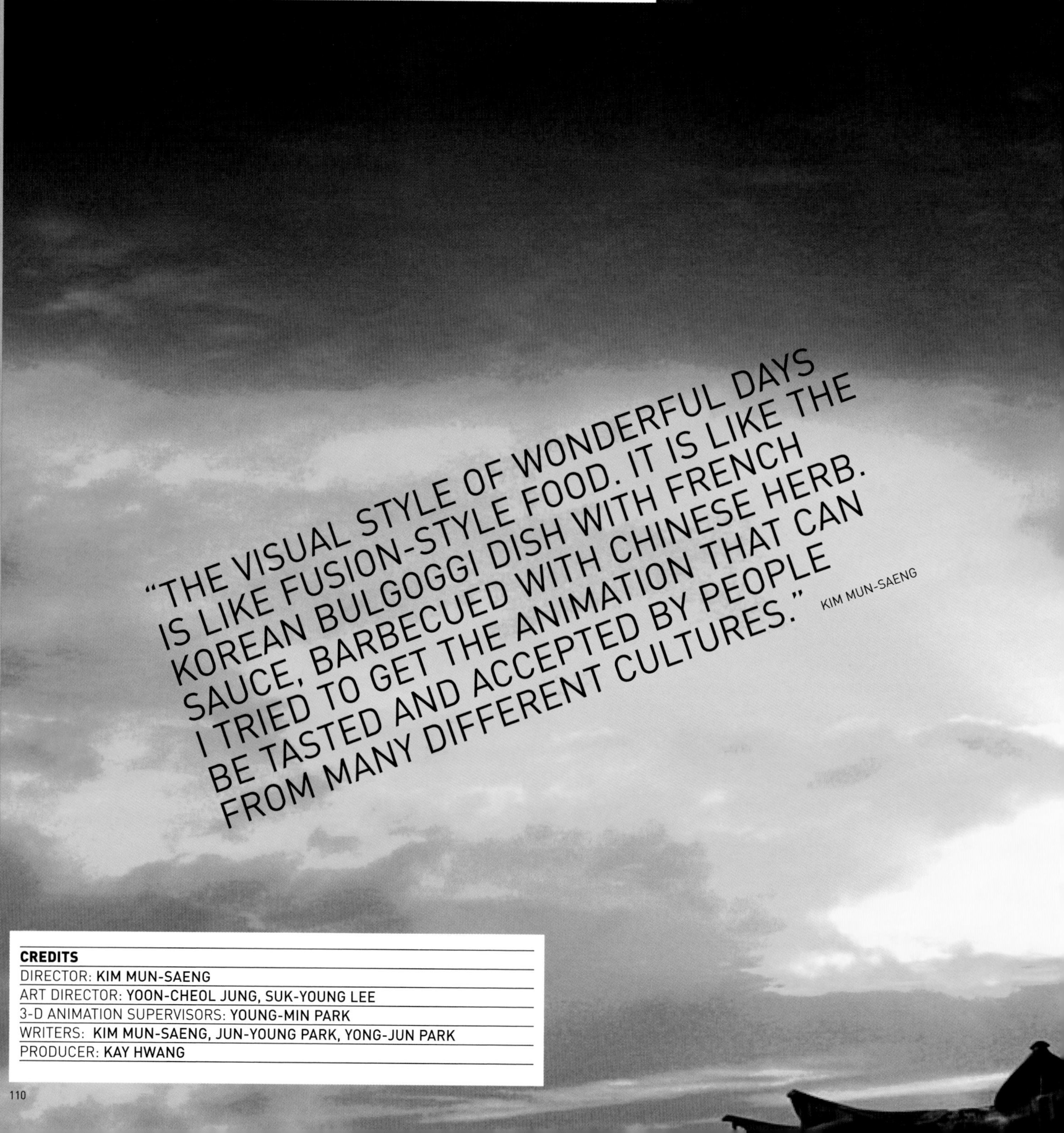

"THE VISUAL STYLE OF WONDERFUL DAYS IS LIKE FUSION-STYLE FOOD. IT IS LIKE THE KOREAN BULGOGGI DISH WITH FRENCH SAUCE, BARBECUED WITH CHINESE HERB. I TRIED TO GET THE ANIMATION THAT CAN BE TASTED AND ACCEPTED BY PEOPLE FROM MANY DIFFERENT CULTURES."

KIM MUN-SAENG

**CREDITS**
DIRECTOR: **KIM MUN-SAENG**
ART DIRECTOR: **YOON-CHEOL JUNG, SUK-YOUNG LEE**
3-D ANIMATION SUPERVISORS: **YOUNG-MIN PARK**
WRITERS: **KIM MUN-SAENG, JUN-YOUNG PARK, YONG-JUN PARK**
PRODUCER: **KAY HWANG**

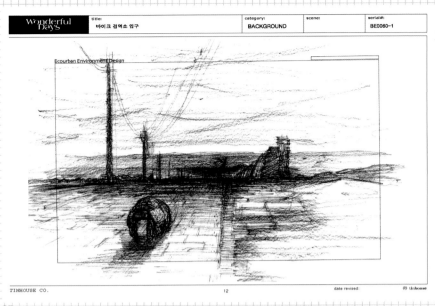

| Wonderful Days | title: 바이크 검역소 입구 | | category: BACKGROUND | scene: | serial#: BE0060-1 |

Ecourban Environment Design

TINHOUSE CO.　　　　　　　12　　　　　　　date revised:　　　　ⓒ tinhouse

02

03

*Wonderful Days* is a spectacularly animated Korean sci-fi eco-thriller, and features an innovative fusion of cel animation, CGI, and miniatures filming. Natural catastrophe has nearly destroyed Earth, brought on by the unfettered pollution and untamed exploitation of the planet's resources. Mankind's last few survivors are divided between an elite who exist within a massive Arcology, the giant, sealed city of Ecoban. Those outside Ecoban—the Marrians—must fend for themselves in the polluted wastelands of the planet.

>>>

IMAGES

01 *Wonderful Days* comprises intricate, hand-painted backgrounds and cutting-edge animation.
02 Environment design sketch.
03 Kim Mun-Saeng: "I was inspired by Metal Hurlant for the characters, Antonio Gaudí for the organic constructions, and traditional Korean pattern designs."

2004
**2003**
2002
2001
2000
1999
1998
1997
1996
1995
1994
1993
1992
1991
1990
1989
1988
1987
1986
1985
1984
1983
1982

Ø1

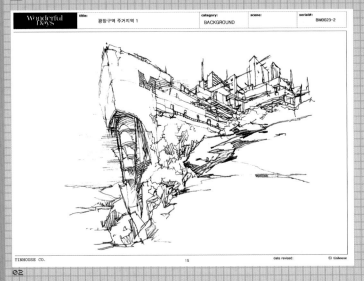

Ø2

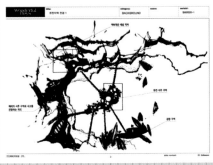

Ø3

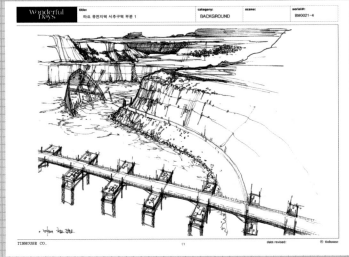

Ø4

## IMAGES

Ø1   Production painting of the Tanker, aground on a dry ocean bed.
Ø2–Ø4  Sketches developing the environment in the Bay Area.
Ø5   Market hide-out in Marr.
Ø6–Ø9  Concept developments for the hide-out illustrate the depth of pre-planning involved in production.

05

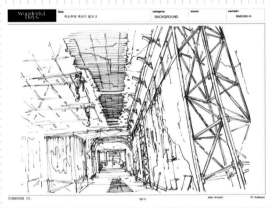

06

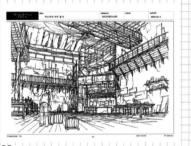

08

07

09

113

2004
2003
2002
2001
2000
1999
1998
1997
1996
1995
1994
1993
1992
1991
1990
1989
1988
1987
1986
1985
1984
1983
1982

Ø1

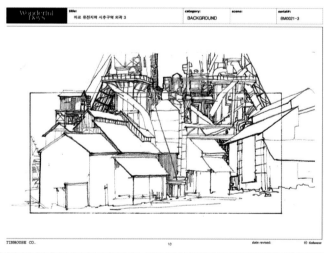

Wonderful
DAYS

| title: 마로 유전지역 시추구역 외곽 3 | | category: BACKGROUND | scene: | serial#: BM0021-3 |

TINHOUSE CO.                    10                    date revised:          ⓒ tinhouse

Ø2

Ø3

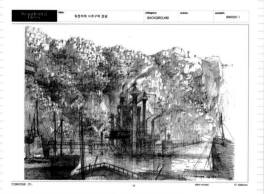

Wonderful
DAYS

| title: 유전지역 시추구역 전경 | | category: BACKGROUND | scene: | serial#: BM0025-1 |

TINHOUSE CO.                    10                    date revised:          ⓒ tinhouse

Ø4

| Wonderful Days | title: 콘트롤라 뮤니트 교각 밑 이미지 | category: BACKGROUND | scene: | serial#: BE0100-1 |
|---|---|---|---|---|

TINHOUSE CO.    16    date revised:    ⓒ Unihouse

06

| Wonderful Days | title: 에코반 입구 도로 2 | category: BACKGROUND | scene: | serial#: BE0090-1 |
|---|---|---|---|---|

TINHOUSE CO.    15    date revised:    ⓒ Unihouse

07

The feature blends stock sci-fi tropes expertly: the apocalyptic outposts à la *Mad Max*, the decaying hide-outs—in this instance, an atmospherically detailed tanker lying beached on a dry ocean bed—and hi-tech fortress city. The Arcology is a highly integrated and dense three-dimensional architectural space. A condensed urban form based on eliminating urban sprawl and waste, ironically, it draws its power from the polluted world outside, through a H.R. Giger-like system of pipes and conduits controlled by the DELOS system. Destruction looms as the Ecobans plan to torch the Marr citystate to generate more pollution to feed their utopian existence—the Marrians must destroy DELOS to avoid this fate.

In recent years, there has been a new emphasis on filmmaking emanating from Korea. While this has mostly focused on live-action feature production, *Wonderful Days* suggests the country's fertile animation industry is raising its game from being simply U.S. television's favorite provider of outsourced animated series. The hybrid style of *Wonderful Days*—combining miniatures filming, matte painting, 2D, and 3D animation styles—is part of a wider movement in Asian special effects, to define a new style of animated filmmaking separate to the hyperreal Hollywood esthetic.

"The input to create combinations of 2D and 3D came from the Director. I agreed with his suggestion, as we wanted to make something different," emphasizes the film's Producer Kay Hwang. "We wanted to make this visually powerful movie, taking full advantage of CGI techniques, as we feel Korea is now developing this technology. Traditionally, Korean movies are very strong on narrative—particularly in drama and comedy—but only a few take advantage of the high-end digital technology available in modern filmmaking. From my point of view, the border between animation and live-action movies is becoming vaguer as CGI develops, which will lead us to new experimental kinds of visual expressions." [1]

>>>

IMAGES

01–04 Concept development of the Marr's frontier city, including the abandoned boatyard.
05–07 A typically ambiguous structure in *Wonderful Days*. The bridge is half cathedral, half modern industrial design.

2004
2003
2002
2001
2000
1999
1998
1997
1996
1995
1994
1993
1992
1991
1990
1989
1988
1987
1986
1985
1984
1983
1982

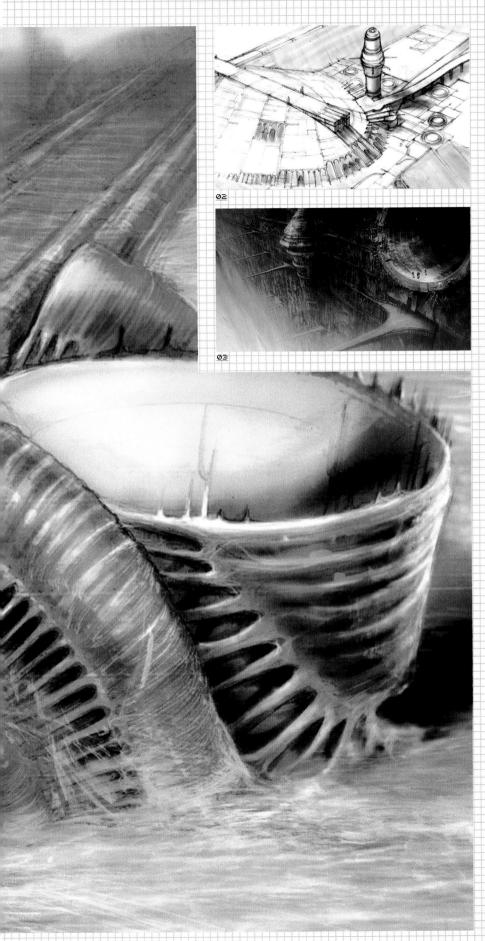

While Hwang cites *Total Recall*, *Star Wars* and *Blade Runner* as well as fiction such as *Neuromancer* (William Gibson, 1985) and *Brave New World* (Aldous Huxley, 1932) as influences, both the Producer and Director were keen to infuse a distinct vision which sought to extend rather than emulate other genre works. They deliberately mixed eastern and western influences: "The visual style of Wonderful Days is explained like fusion-style food," suggests Director Kim. "For example, it is like the Korean Bulgoggi dish with French sauce, barbecued with Chinese herb. I tried to get the animation that can be tasted and accepted by people from many different cultures. I was inspired by *Metal Hurlant* [the influential French comic magazine] for the characters, Gaudi for the organic constructions, as well as traditional Korean pattern designs."

The florid, almost medieval imagery of Ecoban's interior, with monastic interiors and areas recalls the curves of Gaudí's Sagrada Familia Cathedral in Barcelona and the spirals of Frank Lloyd Wright's Guggenheim Museum in New York. The expertly conceived spaces provide visually dazzling set pieces, such as a Mexican stand-off in front of a saturated stained-glass window. Beyond Ecoban, the post-apocalyptic environment takes in such poignant and varied images as a silent, still windfarm, the beached tanker in Bay Area #5, the abandoned boatyard, and Marr's ramshackle frontier outpost.
>>>

IMAGES

01–03 *Alien*-inspired design for Ecoban's pollution filtering system.

2004
2003
2002
2001
2000
1999
1998
1997
1996
1995
1994
1993
1992
1991
1990
1989
1988
1987
1986
1985
1984
1983
1982

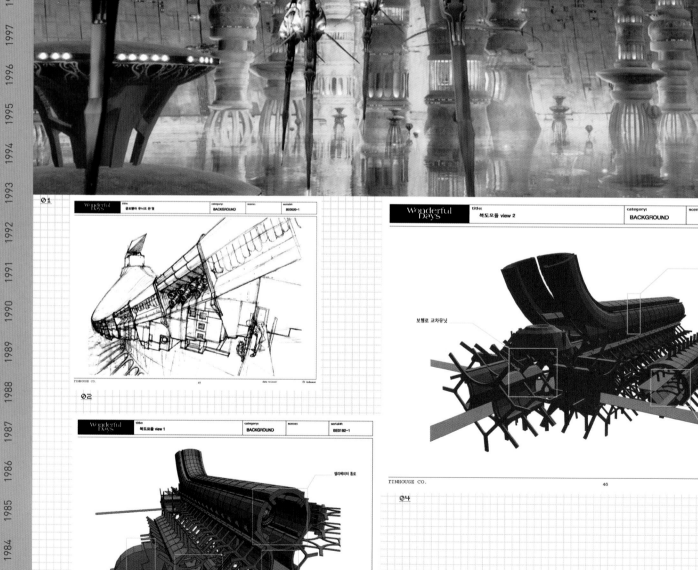

01

| Wonderful Days | 글로벌라 유니트 전 명 | category: BACKGROUND | scene: | serial#: BE0020-1 |

TINHOUSE CO.    49    date revised:    © tinhouse

02

| Wonderful Days | title: 복도모듈 view 1 | category: BACKGROUND | scene: | serial#: BE0192-1 |

엘리베이터 통로
보행자동로3
보행자동로1,2
주거모듈연결유닛

03

TINHOUSE CO.    45    date revised:    © tinhouse

| Wonderful Days | title: 복도모듈 view 2 | category: BACKGROUND | scene: | serial#: BE0192-2 |

엘리베이터 통로
보행로 교차유닛
연결유닛
보행자 통로

TINHOUSE CO.    46    date revised:

04

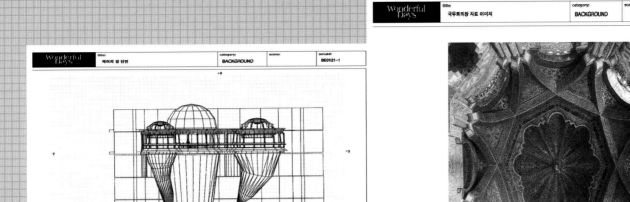

| Wonderful Days | title: 국무회의장 자료 이미지 | category: BACKGROUND | scene: | serial#: BE0235-1 |

TINHOUSE CO.　　　　　84　　　　　date revised:　　　⊕ tinhouse

06

| Wonderful Days | title: 제이의 방 단면 | category: BACKGROUND | scene: | serial#: BE0121-1 |

TINHOUSE CO.　　19　　　date revised:　　⊕ tinhouse

05

| Wonderful Days | title: 제이의 방 자료 이미지 | category: BACKGROUND | scene: | serial#: BE0129-1 |

TINHOUSE CO.　　　　　29　　　　　date revised:　　　⊕ tinhouse

07

| | | category: BACKGROUND | scene: | serial#: BE0201-2 |

TINHOUSE CO.　　　　　50　　　　　date revised:　　　⊕ tinhouse

08

### IMAGES

01　The ornate arcology of Ecoban.
02-04　Ecoban infrastructure sketch and models.
05-08　Model and reference material for Ecoban's exterior and interior detailing, including Renaissance and modern influences, from Gaudí to Frank Lloyd Wright.

2004
**2003**
2002
2001
2000
1999
1998
1997
1996
1995
1994
1993
1992
1991
1990
1989
1988
1987
1986
1985
1984
1983
1982

02

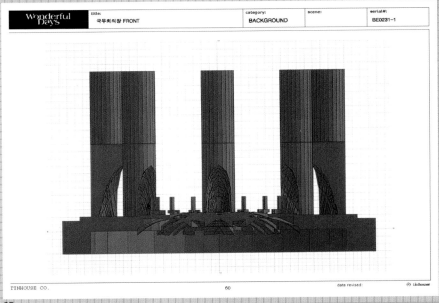

| Wonderful Days | title:<br>국무회의장 FRONT | category:<br>BACKGROUND | scene: | serial#:<br>BE0231-1 |
| --- | --- | --- | --- | --- |

TINHOUSE CO.                                    60                    date revised:              (t) tinhouse

03

To create this evocative landscape, the production used the high-definition Sony HDW-F900 camera, only the second production to do so after Lucasfilms' *Star Wars: Episode 2*. They took advantage of Panavision's Frazier Lens for framing miniatures with a narrow aperture, enabling them to focus on near objects while also taking in background elements. Milo, a motion-control robot was used to match miniatures footage with 3D virtual camera moves. 3D was used for metallic and mechanical elements in the film to emphasize their structure, and CG was also applied to Ecoban city and other large-scale locations. Matte paintings were used to enhance CGI backgrounds, and afford a more dream-like quality. Blending 2D characters into these environments allowed a more "life-like" rendering to enhance the merging of these different methods and cartoon rendering to diffuse hard edges. Selected inking of frames helped bind image elements together into a whole that the production dubbed "multimation."

"We are at the beginning stage for Korean science fiction, so it's too early to speak about the difference between this and Japanese or Western. However, *Wonderful Days* focuses more on the relationship and communication among humans, instead of fighting enemy aliens or monsters," explains Hwang. Particularly as the movie draws to a conclusion, and enters a more abstract realm, reminiscent of Kubrick's *2001*, we can sense the ambition and stretching-for-epic scale in this film. In the climactic battle, as gravity gives way, blood free-floats poetically from characters, echoing the flying blocks within the DELOS system that constantly reconfigure and reform into different structures. *Wonderful Days'* greatest achievement is in the euphoric exploration of its future environment, spaces that are also elegiac and elegant.

IMAGES

01-03 Various production sketches of Ecoban's council chamber, exploring form, material, color, lighting, and scale.

2004
2003
2002
2001
2000
1999
1998
1997
1996
1995
1994
1993
1992
1991
1990
1989
1988
1987
1986
1985
1984
1983
1982

FILM

# NATURAL CITY

## VISUAL EFFECTS

+ **MACOD & MDM USING LIGHTWAVE, 3D STUDIO MAX, AFTER EFFECTS, & INFERNO SOFTWARE**

Ø1

Ø2

Ø3

Ø4

Korean science fiction is booming, but as the genre attempts to find its own particular style, it pillages the best of the rest of the world's offerings to make some fascinating yet flawed movies. *Natural City* is the stand-out live-action sci-fi so far created by this new wave of Korean cinema. Music video alumni Byung-Chin Min wrote, directed, and shot this visually sumptious, incredibly melodramatic feature film.

The movie is an amalgam of *Blade Runner* (see page 18) and more contemporary brethren, such as *Equilibrium* (2002), *Avalon* (2001), and *The Matrix* (see page 104). Byung-Chin Min freely admits *Blade Runner* was the jumping off point to creating this film. Such unrestrained borrowing is clearly evident in obvious narrative parallels. Instead of Replicants we have Combiners, artificially intelligent human clones hard-coded with an expiry date. Naturally, they want to resist this imposed sell-by date for being "recycled." The tropes of tech-noir sci-fi are all here: the megacorporation, gene-modification, fascistic armed forces, sinister machines.

The world has been reconfigured as a series of citystates by 2080, with continuing wars between these factions. The action takes place in and around one such citystate, Mecaline City. The imagery conveyed in Mecaline City is twenty-first century dsytopic modern: not as cluttered, decaying, or grimy, as *Blade Runner*, but an evolution. The L.A. of the future lifted from this genre classic, crossed with an extrapolated Gangnam-gu, the high-rise area of Seoul. Mecaline's city districts move between New York-inspired Warehouse districts, Hong Kong's Causeway Bay, and Kowloon-inspired shacks hovering over the water in the slum district of Raiha.

Art Director Cho Hwa-Seong comes up with some fabulous set designs, including a hauntingly beatiful statue that overlooks the hazy metropolis of Mecaline City. Modish design infuses much of the feature—everything from the motion design of credits, to the jumbled towering mass cityscape is artfully constructed, with restrained use of CG to give futuristic flourishes such as the odd flying car and spaceship. They might not be able to tell a captivating story just yet, but *Natural City* shows the Koreans can definitely paint a pretty picture.

---

**CREDITS**
DIRECTOR: **BYUNG-CHIN MIN**
PRODUCTION DESIGN: **HWA-SEONG CHO**
SCREENPLAY: **BYUNG-CHIN MIN**
VISUAL EFFECTS SUPERVISOR: **DO-AHN JUNG**

05

### IMAGES

01—02 Blues and ambers strikingly color-code *Natural City*.

03 *Blade Runner* without the haze.

04 Cho Hwa-Seong's production design is eclectic and referential, ranging from future modern to that of apocalyptic disaster.

05 3D model of Samsung Tower Palace in Seoul—the largest residential towers in the world—shows the real-world references of the filmmakers.

**FILM**

**VISUAL EFFECTS**

# i, ROBOT

+

**DIGITAL DOMAIN, WETA DIGITAL, RAINMAKER, DIGITAL PICTURES, PIXEL LIBERATION FRONT**

Ø1

Ø2

Ø3

Ø4

A near-future Chicago of 2035 is the setting for the 2004 blockbuster summer sci-fi, *i, Robot*. The production designer, Patrick Tatopoulos, explains its genesis: "The process of preproduction on this picture was almost three years altogether, which is not usual. Alex Proyas, the Director, first came to me when the film was to be called "Hardwired." During the course of developing the story, the Isaac Asimov elements were added into the mix more concretely, which the studio liked because it was maybe creating a franchise opportunity.

It was difficult to get going because it was a "medium" picture. I think the studios like small budgeted pictures or large ones that have a big star so they can bank on getting lots of people to see it. Getting Will Smith on board changed the production into a blockbuster, so the scale of everything changed." [1]

>>>

**IMAGES**

Ø1, Ø5  Concept paintings of future Chicago by Stephan Martinière developed: "From conversation, mainly. Patrick gives me some very loose sketches as well as photographic references for either material ideas or just feel."
Ø2–Ø4  The U.S.R building is the focal point—"the blade of light"— in *i, Robot*.

**CREDITS**

DIRECTOR: **ALEX PROYAS**

PRODUCTION DESIGNER: **PATRICK TATOPOULOS**

SCREENPLAY: **JEFF VINTAR, AKIVA GOLDSMAN**

SCREEN STORY: **JEFF VINTAR**

SUGGESTED BY THE BOOK BY: **ISAAC ASIMOV**

PRODUCERS: **JOHN DAVIS, TOPHER DOW, WYCK GODFREY, LAURENCE MARK**

"FOR ME, THE DESIGN MUST ALWAYS HAVE A GROUNDING IN THE REAL WORLD. WE ALL MAKE OUR OWN LIMITS, AND I WANT TO KEEP IT AS BELIEVABLE AS POSSIBLE." PATRICK TATOPOULOS

2004
2003
2002
2001
2000
1999
1998
1997
1996
1995
1994
1993
1992
1991
1990
1989
1988
1987
1986
1985
1984
1983
1982

01

02

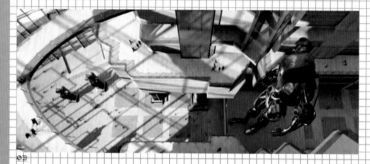

03

04

05

"I LOVED THE IDEA OF TRANSLUCENCY. IT WAS A
WAY TO EVOKE THE FUTURE. THE TREND IN PUBLIC
ARCHITECTURE IS TO BE MORE TRANSPARENT, OPEN,
AND WELCOMING. SO A REAL TOUCHSTONE FOR ME WAS
THE WORK OF SANTIAGO CALATRAVA... ZAHA HADID WAS
ALSO MIXED INTO THIS IDEA." PATRICK TATOPOULOS

IMAGES

01–04  Interior detailing of the U.S.R headquarters.
05  Santiago Calatrava architectural ideas involving translucency had a huge
influence on the film's production design. The Milwaukee Art Museum photograph
highlights the resemblance.
06  Production painting of VICKI (again by Martinière), the U.S.R building's
positronic brain which hangs from the central atrium.

When Tatopoulos first started developing the
production's design, Director Alex Proyas wanted
to shoot the film in Sydney. Tatopoulos had been
scoping Sydney's Olympic Stadium and other
locales in the city, scouting locations for a movie
that was to be set 80 years into the future. As
the situation evolved, *Star Wars* took over the
studio stages, pushing out the possibility of
producing the film in Australia. "Will Smith
changed the scale of the production, and made
it into a more optimistic film with less of the
atmosphere-building Alex would normally
do," says Tatopoulos. "So it was to be more
plot-driven. Smith also wanted to be nearer
his family, so the production had to be nearer to
home, too. All these factors meant we decided
to shoot in Vancouver."

Getting the look of the picture right meant
focusing from the very beginning on the look
of the robot. As one of the lead characters,
everyone knew its design would make or break
the film. This meant eventually going through
over 50 design iterations. Tatopoulos
remembers: "From the robot, Sonny, the whole
theme of the production design came along, like
a chain reaction." This new type of robot, the
NS-5, is central to the film's story. The firm
U.S.R (U.S. Robotics) is about to roll out their
new robot into the world, when one of them
becomes the prime suspect in a murder being
investigated by Detective Spooner (Will Smith)
of the Chicago Police Department.

>>>

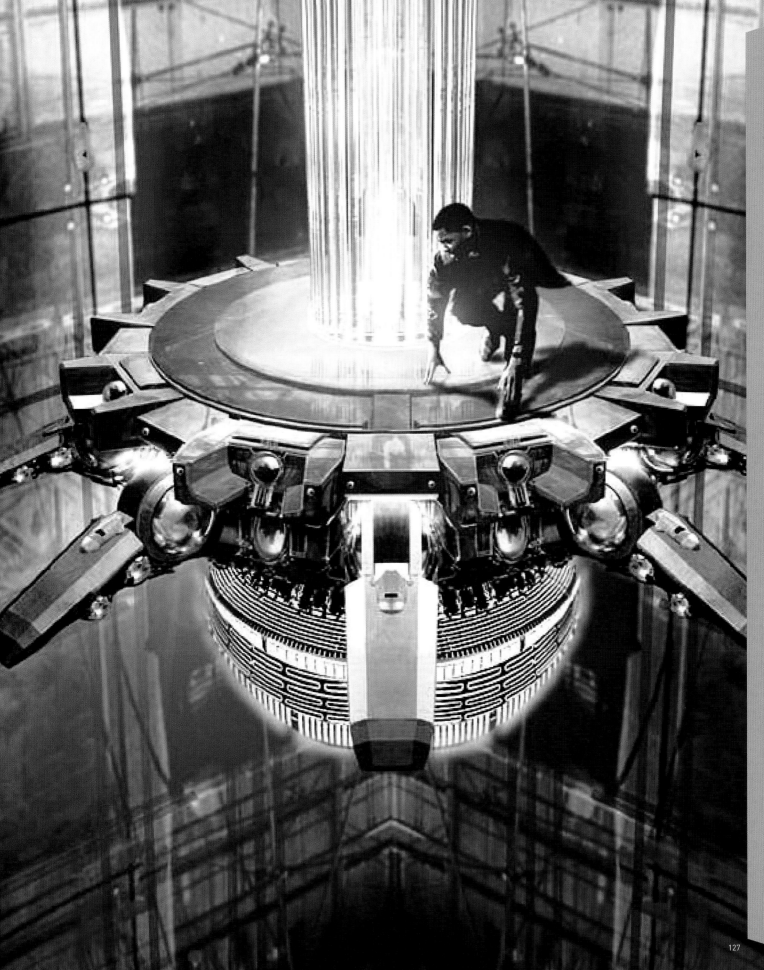

2004
2003
2002
2001
2000
1999
1998
1997
1996
1995
1994
1993
1992
1991
1990
1989
1988
1987
1986
1985
1984
1983
1982

Ø1

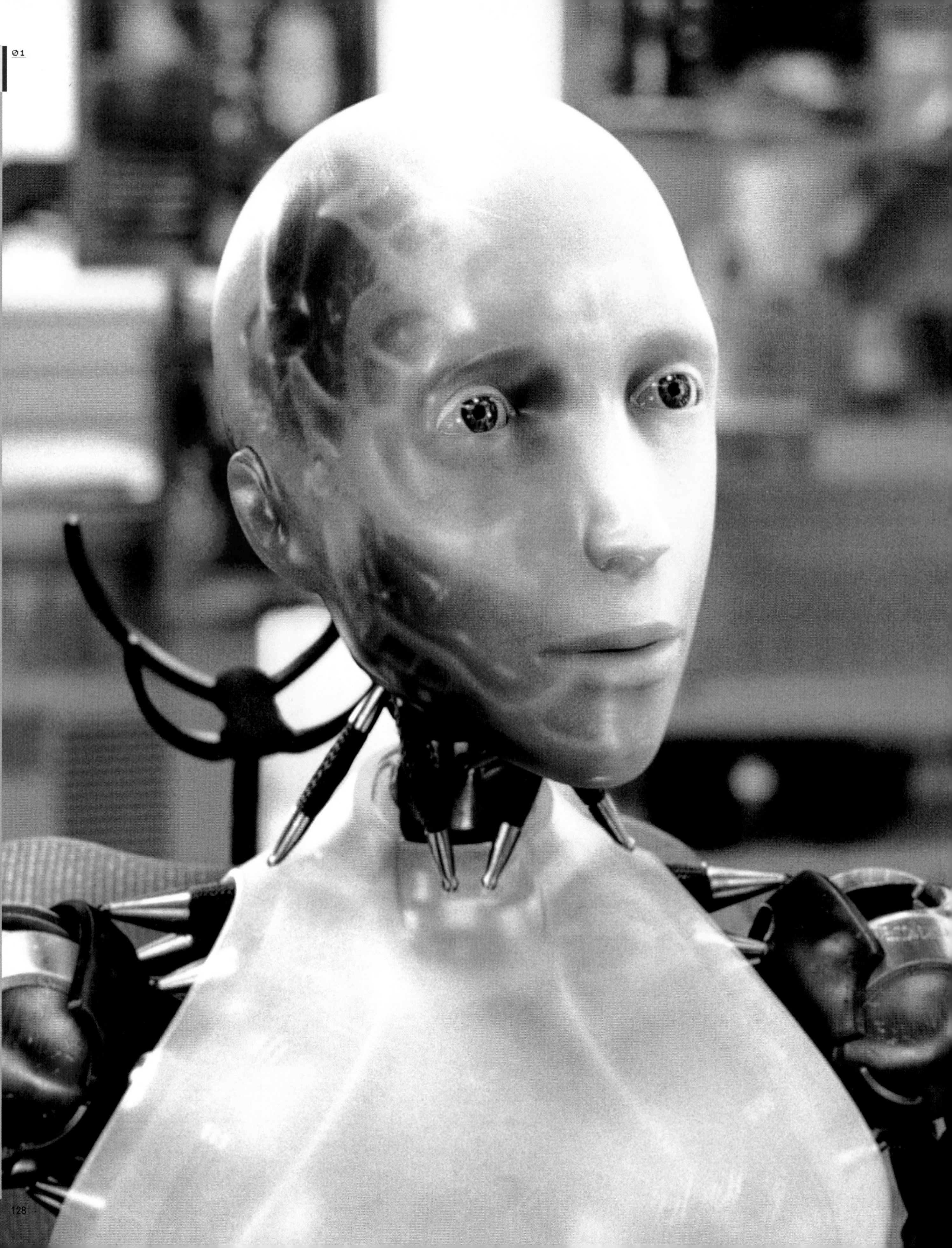

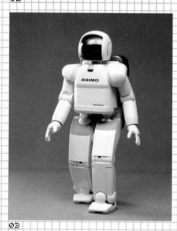

"The transparency theme in the film all came from the idea of the robot. We wanted to get away from this image of it as a Terminator, by making it organic, a lifestyle item," says Tatoupolos. "Twenty years ago, what were computers like? Beige, boring boxes. I'm a big fan of the Apple Mac, so it was obvious to look at what they had done with the iMac, and concentrate on the design rather than the utilitarian aspect of it. So I looked at Honda's Asimo, and thought, in 30 years that's going to be sleeker, more lifestyle. They are going to be smaller, more tightly compact, muscular. People say there's a similarity to our robot and the one in the Björk video for 'All is full of love,' but this one keeps away from pistons and anything too mechanical. We used the same stuff in the design as they are making artificial limbs from now, an elastic 'artificial muscle.'"

As the film changed, the studio also wanted to change the original background of the story. They drew it back to a near future only 30 years ahead, rather than the 80 originally envisaged. "They wanted the audience to be able to relate more, and make it easier on the budget," explains Tatopoulos.

To capture a world populated by humans and robots, the production used a special camera from Digital Domain called Robo-Tile. This takes multiple pictures of a scene from extreme underexposure to extreme overexposure. These pictures are used to generate dynamic range lighting, and are then applied to light digitally created environments and characters.

Virtually all the central U.S.R building was built using CGI: "It took four months to create a full 3D model and an accompanying set. We modeled the whole building digitally. Personally, I'd never done a job like this, where we actually built more of the building than you see in the movie. I just got into the detailing, and that came through in other aspects of the design.

"Alex gave us the guideline for the emphasis he wanted to place on particular aspects of the building. So, in the case of the Atrium, he wanted it very tall and spacious. This pretty much made us decide to create most of the Atrium with digital effects. We built small sections of the building, basically creating a physical patchwork of the building so the actors could operate in it. We also built the penthouse office, which was kind of separate to the rest of the building, some of the catwalk on top of building, the hanging column that drops down from this which holds VICKI (the building's positronic brain), along with the robot lab. The catwalk that we filmed was basically ten feet off the ground. The glass, the city beyond, and everything else, was digital, because, as soon as you start working with so many elements, it's easier to make the glass digital."

>>>

IMAGES

01 Sonny was the film's key design element from which everything else stemmed. To make sure it was exactly right, Tatopoulos went through over 50 design iterations.
02–03 The muscular metal structure of the NS-5 is *i,Robot*'s interpretation of how current models such as the humanoid Honda Asimo will develop.
04 A legion of NS-5s. The semi-transparent shell was sparked by Jonathan Ives' iconic iMac design.

2004
2003
2002
2001
2000
1999
1998
1997
1996
1995
1994
1993
1992
1991
1990
1989
1988
1987
1986
1985
1984
1983
1982

Ø1

Ø2

The sleek creation of U.S.R's corporate headquarters is an integral anchor in creating the two separate design flavors the director required: Firstly, a downtown area—a beautiful metropolitan landscape where large, clean, white plazas are broken up by shiny glass buildings radiating opulence and wealth; secondly, the grungy surburbs.

"I THINK THE BEST DESIGN IS SYNTHESIZING ALL THE INFLUENCES YOU HAVE INTO A WHOLE THAT WORKS. FROM THAT POINT IT IS A QUESTION OF 'HOW DO YOU ENGINEER THIS?'"

PATRICK TATOPOULOS

03

"I loved the idea of translucency. It was a way to evoke the future. The trend in public architecture is to be more transparent, open, and welcoming. So a real touchstone for me was the work of Santiago Calatrava. He is my hero in architecture. He was a real influence on this film because his language is transparency. This generated the framework for coming up with the overall feel of the film's buildings. He utilizes the practicality of the construction process to make his buildings more beautiful. I must say Zaha Hadid was also mixed into this idea. I like bold strokes of the brush, things that are dynamic and interactive. Both these architects put that into their work. You can see the intelligence in the 3D objects they create. So the idea of the U.S.R building came out of that, as a bold brushstroke through the city. It's knife-like, a blade—which gives it a sense of the danger coming from it too. I think the best design is synthesizing all the influences you have into a whole that works. From that point it is a question of 'how do you engineer this?'"

Chicago was chosen to situate the film because it has classic and modern looks, tall, brand-new buildings situated next to projects constructed 50 years ago. It adheres to Proyas' original concept. But it was a challenge recreating this in Vancover. "I like Vancouver but it was the worst choice to recreate this future Chicago. It had too many trees both outside and inside buildings. Part of Alex's stylistic language is to have cities completely without trees. The suburb was easy, as we just built a couple of storefronts, and dressed up some ordinary buildings, pretty similar to what we have normally. We were asked for a typical, tacky, unsexy suburb, and that's what it is. It is a good contrast to the clean, corporate environments where the rest of the action takes place."

The plaza outside the U.S.R Building represented Proyas' idea of power: "When you have power, you're not going to make a taller building, you're going to create a bigger plaza around your building, because the ground is what is expensive."

>>>

IMAGES

01-03 Stephan Martinière's production paintings were essential guides for set dressing, and visual effects design. "The process is very similar for each illustration," he remarks. "I start from either a loose sketch given to me by Patrick or one that I create. Once the sketch is approved, Patrick and I discuss the mood, color palette, and texture, to be used in the illustration. From there, I go directly to a detail painting which takes me a week or two to produce. Patrick knows how I work, and has always been comfortable waiting until the painting is almost at a final stage. Since my paintings are done digitally, in layers, it is easy to make changes at a late stage."[3]

01

02

03

I ROBOT. WASTELAND                    STEPHAN MARTINERE 2003

04

The production department used CGI to enhance the location shooting to achieve Proyas' vision of this affluent urban space. "The problem with CGI is that there are so many possibilities now," elucidates Tatopoulos. "You never have time to push them as far as possible, but people's expectations have been raised to such a level that you have to deliver the goods. Everyone is ambitious about producing standout shots, but then if other aspects have to be rushed to complete the movie in time for a schedule, for release in the summer or whatever, then they can let the film down. It is difficult to integrate the fine, beautiful detail in everything."

Joe Letteri of Weta Digital was charged with coming up with some of this detail within the crammed time frame. He created the futuristic Chicago cityscape based on Tatopoulos's art department production paintings. "We built about 30 high-resolution buildings for the foreground. In the mid-ground, we had medium-resolution buildings that were built from pieces of the main structures. By reorganizing the pieces and moving the buildings around, our cityscape would never look the same." [2]

To help Alex Proyas visualize and direct the action within this digitally augmented environment, the production utilized Encodacam, a technology originally developed but never used on the *Matrix* sequels by Los Angeles-based General Lift. This generates realtime computer graphics from stored 3D models and matches them up on a monitor to what the camera is pointing at on set. It gives the director much more of an idea of the finished equation after postproduction effects have been added to the live action.

Ultimately, these effects helped enhance a reality which Proyas wanted to suffuse the whole production with, a sense that this was a documentary of the future. "I wanted to create a strong sense of reality so that you believe that you're in this world populated by robots," Proyas states. "We've gone with a believable and realistic view of the future. I didn't want to have flying cars and stuff that other people have had in their cinematic visions of the future. I wanted it to feel like it was a real and natural 30-year progression from our world."

*i, Robot* offers a highly believable vision of the future successfully breaking away from the future noir vocabulary of the slew of *Blade Runner* copycats, or the expressionistic course of Proyas' earlier *Dark City* (see page 68). The film takes its design cues from the ultra-modern, from the sleekest industrial design to the most modish architecture.

"Truthfully, when I heard *Minority Report* was gearing up for production, I was slightly fearful because I thought they'd be gathering similar ideas to us. Our mission was to be fairly realistic, based on moving the science forward. We were thinking of conceiving the film from the point of view of a documentary of the future. In terms of what to bring to the table, Alex had artistic licence. It is not a radically new vision, but we did add things to make it more fun, while still situating it in the same world. I came up with the ballwheels on the vehicles such as the U.S.R transporters and Spooner's car, as an odd, interesting touch."

*I, Robot* is evolutionary sci-fi positing a tomorrow that feels highly immediate, because we can see the advances it features beginning to happen now. Like *The Matrix*, this movie's view of the inevitable emergence of artificial intelligence is heavily influenced by *The Age of the Spiritual Machine* (1999), the seminal book by Ray Kurzweil. It belongs to an increasingly dominant sub-genre of sci-fi that accelerates only a number of elements of our normal world into the future, to make it more immediately contemporary. Tatopoulos concludes: "For me, the design must always have a grounding in the real world. We all make our own limits, and I want to keep it as believable as possible."

[ SOURCES ]

[1] PATRICK TATOPOULOS, ORIGINAL INTERVIEW, MATT HANSON (09/2004)

[2] "JOE LETTERI, I, ROBOT AND THE FUTURE OF DIGITAL EFFECTS," ALAIN BIELIK, *VFXWorld* (07/2004)

[3] STEPHAN MARTINIÈRE, ORIGINAL INTERVIEW, MATT HANSON, (10/2004)

IMAGES

01  A finished frame of near-future Chicago.
02–04  Stills and original production painting of the wasteland, situated in the dry bed of what was Lake Michigan. "They had written this part of the action to take place in some non-descript hangars," explains Tatopoulos. "So we went to see some hangars, and they were pretty boring—what can you do with hangars? So we had the idea of using freight containers. Not only are they cheap, because everybody uses them, but they brought with them the idea of robots being shipped all around the world. So a wasteland replaced the hangars, which also added this maze-like flavor to the whole thing, giving it an extra dimension of interest to shoot in. We had four-container-tall sections, and about 250 in total. Then the CG was added to multiply that number. I'm really happy with how this all turned out because Alex used the idea and it fitted in really great with his visual signature."

2004

2003
2002
2001
2000
1999
1998
1997
1996
1995
1994
1993
1992
1991
1990
1989
1988
1987
1986
1985
1984
1983
1982

**FILM**

# APPLESEED

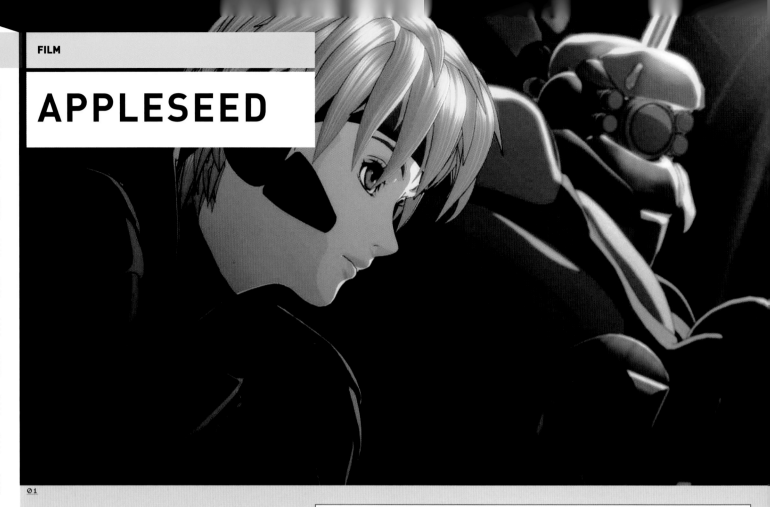

Ø1

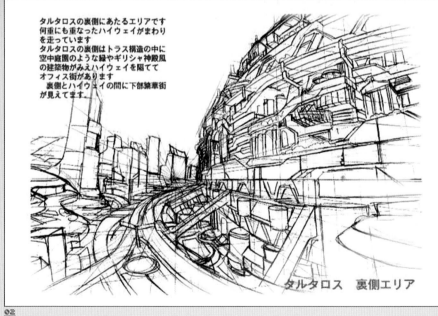

タルタロスの裏側にあたるエリアです
何重にも重なったハイウェイがまわり
を走っています
タルタロスの裏側はトラス構造の中に
空中庭園のような緑やギリシャ神殿風
の建築物がみえハイウェイを隔てて
オフィス街があります
　裏側とハイウェイの間に下部繁華街
が見えてます。

タルタロス　裏側エリア

Ø2

**CREDITS**

DIRECTOR: SHINJI ARAMAKI
PRODUCTION DESIGNER: YOHEI TANEDA
SCREENPLAY: HARUKA HANDA, TSUTOMU KAMISHIRO
COMIC: MASAMUNE SHIROW
SPECIAL EFFECTS SUPERVISOR: HIROYUKI HAYASHI
PRODUCER: FUMIHIKO SORI

03

Comic book artist Masamune Shirow has been an influential presence in Japanese science fiction with movie adaptations of his manga, *Ghost in the Shell* (1995), its sequel Innocence: *Ghost in the Shell 2* (see page 160), and *Appleseed*. These films have all pushed the animated techniques of the time, but with both *Appleseed* and *Innocence*, these limits are being stretched— 2D and 3D techniques are used to create hyperreal cartoon renderings of Shirow's imagined futures.

Billed by the film's producer Fumihiko Sori (who was heavily involved in the digital effects for *Titanic*) as the first film to use a technique called "3D live animé," it utilizes motion capture to render fluid, lifelike character animation. The movie is completely comprised of cel-shaded CGI for the characters, with structures and mecha generated with 3D shading.

*Appleseed* showcases an environment in 2131. Olympus City is a utopian sanctuary from the devastation created by World War III. The remaining members of the human race are locked in a war with bioroids, an army of machines who once were domestic servants. The backdrop of this model city evokes the arcadian fantasies of the contemporary ideals of what a future city should be. It is as if the shimmering towers of Tokyo's glamorous Roppongi Hills development have been cloned and refined for another century. For its perfectionist slant, *Appleseed* is surprisingly unusual, in a genre that likes the nightmarish, the fanciful, and the apocalyptic.

04

05

06

IMAGES

01 *Appleseed* features motion-captured animated performances from its main characters.
02–03 Drawing studies of urban environments.
04–06 The gleaming utopia of Olympic City under attack.

**FILM**

**VISUAL EFFECTS**

# IMMORTEL

+ **DURAN**
**SOFTWARE: DUTREC, LIGHTWAVE, MAYA, CUSTOM SOFTWARE**

Ø1

**CREDITS**
DIRECTOR: ENKI BILAL
PRODUCTION DESIGNER: JEAN-PIERRE FOUILLET
WRITING CREDITS: BASED ON THE COMIC BOOKS LA FOIRE AUX IMMORTELS AND LA FEMME PIÈGE BY ENKI BILAL
STORY, SCREENPLAY AND DIALOG: ENKI BILAL
STORY AND SCREENPLAY: SERGE LEHMAN
PRODUCERS: CHARLES GASSOT, DANIEL J. WALKER
VISUAL EFFECTS SUPERVISOR: JACQUEMIN PIEL, SEB CAUDRON

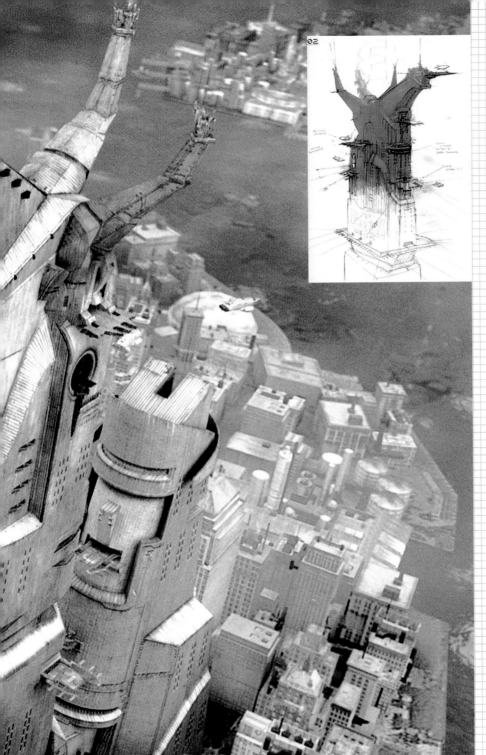

In Director Enki Bilal's science fiction vision, the New York of 2095 has been transformed into a baroque metropolis, combining elements from a knowing mélange of genre sources. Embedded in the film's genetic code, we can find traces of *Blade Runner* (see page 18), *Dark City* (see page 68), *The Fifth Element* (see page 60), and other contemporary sci-fi, as well as Egyptian mythology, and the unmistakable influences of Europe's best graphic novels. Indeed, Belgrade-born artist Bilal can claim to be amongst Europe's leading artists in the form, alongside Moebius (Jean Giraud), Hergé, and René Goscinny. It was Goscinny who actually encouraged Bilal to work on "bande dessinée" (the French term for comic strips) when he met him in his early teens, and Bilal contributed to Goscinny's influential *Pilote* magazine.

*Immortel* is a visually rich story which starts with the potent image of a giant pyramid hovering over Manhattan. Inhabited, unbeknown to New York's citizens, by a number of ancient Egyptian gods, the structure is a bold and evocative image above the city. Hawk-headed god of the sun, Horus, has conjured a way to escape a death sentence exacted upon him by his fellow gods, and so must search the city for a girl who is able to mate with an *Immortel*.

The film has a notably Gallic sensibility. An adaptation of Bilal's most famous graphic novels, *La Foire aux Immortels* and *La Femme Piège*, parts of his *Nikopol* trilogy, *Immortel*'s fantastical vision was deemed unfilmable by the Director, until Producer, Charles Gassot, pushed the artist to look at the latest evolutions in computer animation. He decided they could, but in a way far from what we have come to expect visual effects to be used. The photorealist approach of Hollywood's effects shops was to play no part here, the effects would be in service to Bilal's vision, making the pages of his graphic novels come to life.

>>>

IMAGES

01 The Manhattan of *Immortel* is dominated by the towering Eugenics building.
02 Detailed study of the apex of the Eugenics tower.

2004
2003
2002
2001
2000
1999
1998
1997
1996
1995
1994
1993
1992
1991
1990
1989
1988
1987
1986
1985
1984
1983
1982

Ø1

Ø2

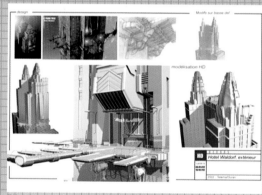

Ø4

Ø3

VOLUME

CODE
NOM  Hotel Waldorf
Designer  P Garcia

NOTA BENE
Validé
23.08.2001

VALIDATION

Ø5

IMAGES

01 *Immortel* brings to life a comic book New York City, humming with in-air traffic.

02–05 Finished stills along with a variety of graphic references for the Hotel Waldorf.

06–11 *Immortel* used exclusively virtual sets, integrating live green screen shots of actors with detailed 3D models and CG backgrounds. "Previsualizing the whole film was the only way to try to offer solutions within our budget, the only way to avoid becoming mad during the shoot," elucidates Visual Effects Superviser Jacquemin Piel. "When you have a team to shoot a movie full of visual effects or 3D, you better keep things under control. Constraints open more creative possibilities. Previs is a good tool between a producer and a director. It allows a proper assessment of the risks."

06

09

07

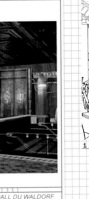

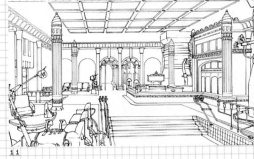
10

intention de texture

HALL DU WALDORF

08

11

"1274 SHOTS WITH 388 SHOTS COMPLETELY ANIMATED IN 3D FOR A TOTAL OF 26 MINUTES; 500 SHOTS MIXING 3D AND 'LIVE ACTION', REPRESENTING 38 MINUTES; AND 280 SHOTS WITH VISUAL EFFECTS AND COMPOSITING REPRESENTING ANOTHER 20 MINUTES." JACQUEMIN PIEL

2004
2003
2002
2001
2000
1999
1998
1997
1996
1995
1994
1993
1992
1991
1990
1989
1988
1987
1986
1985
1984
1983
1982

01

05

02

06

03

07

04

08

## IMAGES

01–08 The most challenging 3D set for Piel: "From my point of view, the sequence where Horus goes out of the pyramid and dives to transform into a falcon before flying towards the city. The 3D effects themselves weren't a technological feat, but combining these with the exterior views was a very good use of the 3D, to give freedom to a director. When Horus sees New York City, the camera tracks back for several kilometers while a helicopter enters the frame at the same moment. This is impossible to achieve in conventional cinema. But, most importantly, in three seconds, it gives a member of the audience the relativity of Horus's size compared to the pyramid, and the size of this pyramid compared to New York. We are really in extremely wide shots."

09 The Egyptian Gods overlooking virtual Manhattan.

10 Signature buildings of *Immortel*— the Pyramid and Eugenics buildings.

1⦶

Duran, the Paris-based effects house responsible for elaborate digital work in films such as *Alien Resurrection* (1997), *The Messenger: The Story of Joan of Arc* (1999), and *Amélie* (2001), was tasked with creating Europe's first "digital backlot" production. Visual Effects Supervisor Jacquemin Piel oversaw the most ambitious digital effects movie undertaken in the region.

"Most of the time, you just need to integrate the special effects as discreetly as possible into the filmed images of the movie," Piel remarks on the usual work approach needed. "In general, the majority of the images are elements shot in 35mm. Here, the challenge was completely different. At the reading of the script, we were really scared. We knew it was an entire movie we had to deal with. Everybody knew Enki's images, these urban landscapes. To us, the Horus character was as well known as Tintin! The tremendous thing was the trust the Director put in us from the beginning.

Duran was in charge of the set design for all the exteriors of NY in 2095, and for the interiors in 3D, such as the metro station. So we had to supervise the design with the artists to create all the buildings, the vehicles. We had to start with all the research, drawing intended light effects, to drawn layouts and, at last, end up with the model sheets. At the meetings, Enki was asking for a pencil and corrected our drawings on tracing paper. It was an advantage to have a Director who can draw. At the same time, Enki didn't wish that we took inspiration from his comic books."[1]

The first European movie entirely digitally composited brought a different set of challenges to those the animation studio had experienced before. It took a team of 100 designers to model, animate, texture, light, and composite the movie over two years. Piel reels off the statistics: "1274 shots with 388 shots completely animated in 3D for a total of 26 minutes; 500 shots mixing 3D and "live action" representing 38 minutes; and 280 shots with visual effects and compositing representing another 20 minutes." Creating a 96-minute movie saturated with special effects on a European budget was an immense technical and artistic challenge. To keep within the budget limitations—reports suggest *Immortel*'s entire budget was around the $20 million mark, a fraction of the price of most Hollywood science fiction—it was essential to previsualize the entire movie, mapping the whole thing in 3D before even a reel of 35mm film was shot in the studio. In this way, the most economical and efficient way to create the finished image could be worked out well in advance.

"Each sequence, each shot, was motion tracked with a 3D camera. We had a special tool developed by the studio to frame each shot with virtual actors evolving in the low-res film set. It was interesting to 'direct' the movie before shooting with the real actors. It allowed us to find solutions to transfer the script into image," explains Piel. The digital workflow evolving from previs included Maya for modeling and animation, while LightWave was utilized for rendering. Compositing and 2D work used their proprietary solution, Dutruc.

>>>

141

2004
2003
2002
2001
2000
1999
1998
1997
1996
1995
1994
1993
1992
1991
1990
1989
1988
1987
1986
1985
1984
1983
1982

01

Production of effects was aided by the Director explicitly wanting to avoid the photorealistic "Hollywood" style, but rather to create a hybrid, combining live-action, CG work, motion captured performances, and digital animation.

"With Enki, we knew his drawings, his painting," says Piel. "Our work really started when we had to agree on the word 'realism.' Of course, it wasn't real life. But we had to define the light, the materials, the textures of each object, each character. Were the materials going to be painted, were we going to mix real textures, how would the light, and color calibrations work? The possibilities are immense and this is when it becomes complex. With 3D, the director is always tempted to delay the choices. My work was to present Enki with possibilities and, little by little, to make him validate the steps. Fortunately, we also had in mind two masterpieces—*Bladerunner* (see page 18) and *Metropolis*.

Of course, Piel's team had a head start, using Bilal's original source material as a rich base from which to spin-off their inspiration: "The design of the film is quite contemporary. Enki wanted the look of this universe to be based on the past. He felt that it would be more realistic than an out-of-this-world sci-fi environment. For example, he had this idea that Manhattan would look pretty much the same as today, except for some new buildings and for the fact that the whole street level had been raised by 50 stories. In 2095, people walk into buildings at what used to be the 50th floor in our time. The city in *Immortel* has the same street plan as Manhattan, but it's ultimately a Bilal city."[2]

The process of creating the idiosyncratic look of the cityscape was unusual and fluid. Piel and his team created detailed drawings from reference material to reproduce real New York buildings. These were turned into 3D models with minimal detailing and passed on to Bilal, who would work directly on the hard copies to embellish them with his trademark style and idiosyncratic flourishes.

>>>

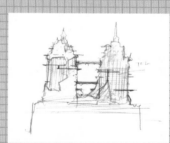

02

03

## IMAGES

**01** *Immortel* takes the classic first generation of New York skyscrapers and accentuates their detailing.
**02–06** Amalgamating New York and Chicago high-rise towers such as the Tribune Tower.
**07–09** Residential blocks like the famous Dakota Apartment Building were used as reference for Eldorado.

04

07

05

08

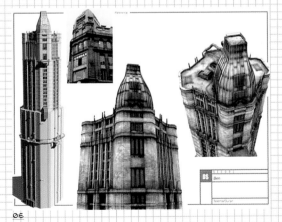

06

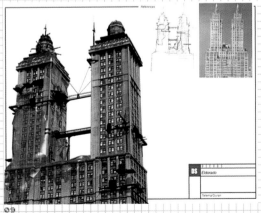

09

2004

2003
2002
2001
2000
1999
1998
1997
1996
1995
1994
1993
1992
1991
1990
1989
1988
1987
1986
1985
1984
1983
1982

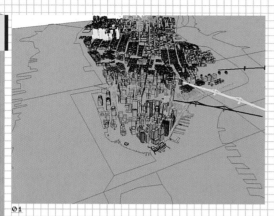

01

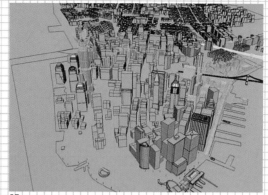

02

03

06

NYDZ (New York Downtown en Zone)

Z15
Z11    Z16
Z12    Z17
Z09         Z18
Z02  Z05  Z06    Z13
Z08    Z03    Z14
Z04    Z07
Z10
Z01

04

05

07

01–05 Effects house Duran created a complete 3D model of Downtown Manhattan. Highlighted areas illustrate highly detailed and texture-mapped zones that feature in fly-throughs and chase scenes.

06–07 *Immortel*'s stunning cityscape. "The biggest challenge was still to create a lot of different sets in a very tight schedule without compromising the quality," states Piel. "That's why we had to be ingenious and to look for the best possible productivity/quality ratio."

2004
2003
2002
2001
2000
1999
1998
1997
1996
1995
1994
1993
1992
1991
1990
1989
1988
1987
1986
1985
1984
1983
1982

Ø1

"This process gave him the opportunity to paint directly on the printouts, adding futuristic or unusual elements to the buildings. When we got them back, the structures were no longer recognizable," explains Piel. "For example, while we may have seen hover cars flying through the skyscraper canyons of Manhattan before, Bilal's vision incorporates a retro-futuristic electric-tram-style wire system which supercharges your journey speed as a sort of expressway through the city.

"Major work started by researching for eight months. We presented lots of architecture from the period between 1880-1930, from Chicago as well as NY, Paris, Prague, or Moscow—famous buildings. From then, an architect started to draw façades for us. 3D graphic designers then had at their disposal a bible selected by Bilal, which was used as reference throughout the project. In this way, around 50 buildings were customized and assembled in districts, linked by footbridges and tunnels. The cable network for the traffic was inserted, with vehicles inspired by 1950s models." These elements, along with judicious use of futuristic flying craft and spaceships, added to the patina of a historically viable city of the future.

Once Bilal approved the myriad environments that were constructed, Duran finalized detailed model sheets to finish creation of all the buildings in appropriate detail, including the monumental Eugenics Building—a fusion of the Chrysler and Empire State—the Hotel Waldorf, and Tycho Brahé bar. Duran's Christine Gatto and Frederic Palacio coordinated the work on these environments.

The Eugenics Building is the centerpiece of this reimagined Manhattan. The muscular column is the signature of *Immortel*'s skyline, even more so than the alien Pyramid. "The Eugenics Building is the center of power and so dominates the city. At design stage, we wanted to tackle this building from the start, as we knew it was at the center of the scenario, so its appearance was going to be essential. Enki's wish, in this instance, was for a completely new creation, without any reference to an existing building. This meant the actual design was the longest to finalize and put in place. After long discussions with Enki on what qualities he wished to give this building—a sense of the strange, for it to be imposing, emanating power—the designer, Renaud Garetta, did several drawings. One of them got Enki moving. Little by little, the Eugenics Building was born."

Current use of CG generally emphasizes verisimilitude above everything else. Duran's assignment was to move against this re-creation of perfect objects and pristine modeling, to inject flaws, imperfections, and, ultimately, engender a quality of otherworldliness more in keeping with this realm.

"3D is often presented as a cold tool, lifeless, synthetic," observes Piel. "Certain movies are impossible to watch, as the image is overly neat, like a chromium-plated, shiny metal. In life, things are damaged, so now we see rust everywhere in certain video games. The important thing is to get the image you want to see at the end. We have always liked to add grain in videos, to 'soil' the image. But nothing prevents us from painting in the textures using the software tools. As soon as you light in 3D, the painting becomes real and this is interesting. Enki asked us to generate a silvery image, like that produced in winter, with a very developed grey gamut. Obviously, the fact we were mixing 3D and live action forced us to respect the original lighting of the shoot."

Inhabiting these virtual environments are a mix of live-action and virtual characters styled in a way we are more used to seeing in video games. This kind of mix polarizes audiences into those who are used to this variety of representations, and the pre-digital audience who cannot get these different looks to gel together in hybrid form.

*Immortel* is to be applauded as a genuinely offbeat creation, an advance from the regular takes on the future. It manages the seemingly impossible in re-visioning the overfamiliar environment of New York into one that is both incredibly unusual and exotic. As a hybrid blend of machinima and live action, the futurist fable marks a refreshing direction in the genre, where the technical wonders of CG are used to create a poetic wide-screen vision.

【 SOURCES 】

[1] JACQUEMIN PIEL, ORIGINAL INTERVIEW, MATT HANSON (09/2004)

[2] "BRINGING THE POWER AND POETRY OF BILAL TO THE BIG SCREEN," ALAIN BIELIK, *VFXWorld* (08/2004)

IMAGES

Ø1 The hovering prison ship of Globus One. Piel: "The most difficult shots to manage were, among others, the 3D sets of the Globus Penitentiary and Manhattan Bridge. Considering these sets were seen at the same time in fine details and in large shot, we faced huge difficulties with the size of the files, and therefore they required enormous preparatory work."
Ø2 Finished frames were treated and colorized to create a stylized look.

**FILM**

# CASSHERN

01

02

03

### CREDITS

DIRECTOR: **KAZUAKI KIRIYA**

PRODUCTION DESIGNER: **YUJI HAYASHIDA**

SCREENPLAY: **KAZUAKI KIRIYA, DAI SATO, SHOTARO SUGA**

SPECIAL EFFECTS SUPERVISOR: **THOSHIYUKI KIMURA**

PRODUCERS: **HIDEJI MIYAJIMA, TOSHIHARU OZAWA, TOHSIAKI WAKABAYASHI**

04

IMAGES

01 *Casshern* is the first true live action steampunk feature film.
02–03 3D models feature constructivist-inspired propaganda posters and monumental face statues.
04 A totalitarian victory parade through the citystreets features hovering war machines.

A turbocharged reimagining, if not complete reinvention of the original manga, *Robot Hunter Casshern*, this film marks the future of science fiction. Kazuaki Kiriya wrote, directed and shot this epic steampunk adventure that distils some of the great visual motifs of the genre into 140 minutes, extracting archetypal narrative set pieces and administering extraordinary battle scenes played out in an apocalyptic landscape.

To many, the ungoverned visual energy will overpower the performances and the melodramatic storyline. But this is meant to be a larger-than-life motion picture, where the primary enjoyment lies in marveling at the invention of this new world. Primarily, film is a visual medium that can too often be hamstrung by the text—*Casshern*'s celebration of spectacle puts that right, and creates an astonishing Asian-flavored sci-fi that currently has no compare.

"After fifty years of bitter warfare, the Eastern Federation has beaten Europa's armies and taken control of the Eurasian continent. Pockets of resistance fighting the oppressive new regime remain in Eurasian Zone Seven..." So begins *Casshern's* convoluted future fable set in an era of totalitarian, warmongering states. Cyrillic and kanji signs litter the urban environments, liberally mixing Russian constructivist, Japanese manga, and Nazi imagery into a unique, highly stylized appearance.

>>>

2004
2003
2002
2001
2000
1999
1998
1997
1996
1995
1994
1993
1992
1991
1990
1989
1988
1987
1986
1985
1984
1983
1982

Ø1

Ø2

08

"We took a lot of visual references from the Russian avant garde," explains Kiriya. "We wanted to create a flat 2-D world, intentionally ignoring the perspectives like in animé. Also, one of our Art Directors is Haruhiko Shono, who created the CD-rom movie, *Gadget*. His vision was truly instrumental... We tried really hard to downgrade the 'digital' feel to achieve the retro look. We didn't want anything slick."[1]

Under the influence of Shono's Victorian-era sci-fi esthetic, *Casshern* rejects the modish tech nouveau evident in other films of the time, to be more mechanical, medieval. The screen is loaded with mechanical war machines powered by cogs, gears, and rotating blades. Robot armies, sternly monolithic architecture, and nightmarish vistas are enhanced by graphic detailing, impressionistic visual effects, and forced perspectives.

Shot on a 24 FPS progressive scan digital camera, the production utilized green screen, a phenomenal amount of CG, and matte paintings. The environment is filtered through blown-up black-and-white film grain, super-saturated colors, and irreal visual effects straight out of video games such as the *Final Fantasy* series. The production of *Casshern* learns from the techniques of videogame visuals production to craft something which is a true hybrid between a cinematic and computer game look. 160 richly textured scenes were created, with the film totaling 3,000 cuts, and costing a miraculous $6 million. It wouldn't be a surprise to see Hollywood spend ten to 20 times that amount to get the same result in an already muted remake.

*Casshern* uses CG to create a realm of electrified senses, a hyperreal zone, that is leading the genre into increasingly fantastical scenarios following the "future documentary" tone of science fiction film at the start of the decade that moved away from the mythical. In doing so, it brings a graphic intensity and broader philosophical exploration to current concerns such as genetic modification, ethnic cleansing, and global terrorism.

IMAGES

01_ Dr Azuma's "neo-cell" laboratory, designed to grow new organs— instead, a freak accident creates Shinzo Ningen, a new superhuman.
02_ Fight scenes abstract the environment in an expressionistic view of the action.
03–07_ Production paintings clearly show the influence of Nazi monumentalism and the Russian avant garde.
08_ Robot armies wage destruction.

[ SOURCE ]

[1] KAZUAKI KIRIYA INTERVIEW, WWW.JOBLO.COM (03/2004)

2004

2003
2002
2001
2000
1999
1998
1997
1996
1995
1994
1993
1992
1991
1990
1989
1988
1987
1986
1985
1984
1983
1982

**FILM**

**VISUAL EFFECTS**

+ INDUSTRIAL LIGHT & MAGIC,
THE ORPHANAGE, LUMA

# SKY CAPTAIN AND THE WORLD OF TOMORROW

**CREDITS**
DIRECTOR: **KERRY CONRAN**
PRODUCTION DESIGNER: **KEVIN CONRAN**
VISUAL EFFECTS SUPERVISOR: **DARIN HOLLINGS**
WRITTEN BY: **KERRY CONRAN**
PRODUCERS: **JON AVNET, JUDE LAW, SADIE FROST, MARSHA OGLESBY**

01

*Sky Captain and the World of Tomorrow* is an unusual film, not only for the pioneering way it was produced—it has earned a place in history as the first Hollywood studio-backed "digital backlot" production—but the fact that it glances back to the past in a genre that is relentlessly forward-facing. *Sky Captain* has a retro sci-fi appeal, based both on the stylized look enabled by the latest digital technologies, and the nostalgia it evokes by harking back to a yesteryear "golden age" of science fiction, to the quintessential sci-fi serial *Flash Gordon*, and *Boy's Own* adventures.

Starting as a short by Director Kerry Conran—he'd been working on the film for four years, incorporating techniques of animation he had learned when he was at Cal Arts—the conversion to blockbuster digital feature was made when Producer Jon Avnet got involved while looking to champion a new talent. Conran initially used Egg (the original name of After Effects before Adobe bought and developed the product) to create the early scenes. The short he built using this new compositing software persuaded Avnet to bankroll development.

Visual Effects Supervisor Darin Hollings got on board as soon as he saw Conran's original take for the project. "I met Kerry in his garage, because that's what they were working out of at the time. He'd got his six-minute short at that point, and after seeing the first couple of scenes, I knew I wanted to be involved. I thought this film had a more artistic slant than what I'd previously been working on, and a lot of potential. I'd seen a few things that had a similar look, such as the video game *Crimson Skies* (2000), but nothing that had really done it justice.

>>>

IMAGES

01 Flying wings straight out of a 1930s sci-fi serial.
02&03 Composite of stylized Manhattan, with background and foreground elements.

2004
2003
2002
2001
2000
1999
1998
1997
1996
1995
1994
1993
1992
1991
1990
1989
1988
1987
1986
1985
1984
1983
1982

Ø1

Ø2

"As soon as I saw what had already been done—showing this world that doesn't exist, that's sci-fi, retro, and high-contrast—I thought that if we could successfully extend this into a full feature, then we'd have something fresh and new. Comparing the original short to the finished film—it was black and white, bold, and very graphic, with almost comic-book style backgrounds, with very contrasting elements—the feature is less edgy, but more watchable. I think it would have been difficult to extend the short using the original look. It would have been harder to watch for such a long period, and been less about the story.

"In the end, the visual style was influenced by Humphrey Bogart films like *To Have and Have Not* (1944). The artistic vision was really driven by Kerry, and my ideas just facilitated his genius. But I had a lot of scope to flesh things out. A lot of the backgrounds I made by just being behind the camera snapping, executing the reference material to bring into compositing, and to aid the creation of the scenes. The Compositing Supervisor, Stephen Lawes, should be credited with bringing a huge contribution to the visuals, as he really worked out how all the filmed and digital elements would go together and marry up on-screen." [1]

Set in 1939, Joe "Sky Captain" Sullivan is tasked with solving the riddle of why famous scientists from around the world are disappearing, and fending off an attack from giant robots in New York City. Together with intrepid reporter Polly Perkins, he must track down the evil Dr. Totenkopf, who plans to wipe out civilization to create a new "World of Tomorrow."

To marry this pulp fiction to the film's stylized look and successfully re-create this period also required an immersion into the cinematic vernacular of the past. "We wanted to keep the suspension of disbelief at hand by referencing this with a comic book adventure as much as possible," continues Hollings. "Right at the start of the film, we have Polly typing, facing the screen, and the type appears behind her, taking up the whole back wall of the office. And we have other recognizable things from the period, like the whirling newspaper montage. If we wanted to re-create a period device, we would just get the movies that had the best examples and then figure out how we could improve on those. We were basically standing on the shoulders of these previous things."

The references for this old-fashioned, art deco-influenced, futuristic period piece were almost single-handedly produced by Kevin Conran, the Director's brother. As the film is a sort of homage to the Republic serials of the past, Conran decided it was best for the film to wear its influences on its sleeve. "The first, of course, is the old Fleischer Brothers' *Superman* cartoons." Fleischer's *Superman* short, *Mechanical Monsters* (1941), inspired the industrial, rivets-and-all conception of all the retro-futuristic contraptions in *Sky Captain*. "But for me, personally, it's Alex Raymond, Raymond Loewy, Norman Bel Geddes, some of the industrial designers from that day... Cheseley Bonestell, Hugh Ferriss... there's a million of them." [2]
>>>

"YOU HAVE TO BE ABLE TO TAKE A STEP BACK AND SCRAP A WHOLE SHOT IF YOU CAN MAKE IT BETTER SOME OTHER WAY. IN PREVIOUS MOVIES, I WAS USED TO DOING SIX TO EIGHT DIFFERENT VERSIONS TO TWEAK A SHOT. IN **SKY CAPTAIN**, WE HAD COMPOSITES WHICH WERE #165-166!"
DARIN HOLLINGS

03

04

05

06

07

08

IMAGES

01 A giant robot.
02 Spoof comic book cover for the movie.
03–05 Blue screen, black and white, and colorized elements illustrate the different stages of the image production process.
06–08 Giant robots invade a virtual Manhattan, with all-live elements shot on stage and matched to animation. Darin Hollings explains how they prepared: "I went on two production trips to New York with DP Eric Adkins. We found a street in Tribeca we liked that was about the right height and had a good look, then we documented it, measuring size, and taking orthographic photographs with as long a lens as possible to minimize perspective distortion. We collected visual material such as textures to pass on to the modelers and texture mappers to build everything in 3D. This is how I could drive the look of a scene."

2004

2003
2002
2001
2000
1999
1998
1997
1996
1995
1994
1993
1992
1991
1990
1989
1988
1987
1986
1985
1984
1983
1982

01

02

03

This hermetic approach allowed a distinctive look to develop worlds away from the prevailing esthetics of future minimalism or industrial cyberpunk, harking back to those pulp sci-fi serials of the 1930s and 1940s. "This is sort of Buck Rogers," explains Conran. "Those serials had cliff-hangers, and that's what this is. For film lovers, there are a lot of references in there that will go by pretty quickly and there are definite elements of homage, but they're not done in a way to say, 'Oh, look at this as a homage.' It's in the 1930s and the music of the 1930s, the costume of the 1930s. We like the retro. We like the art deco." [3]

Conran predicted to Hollings that 70 percent of the movie backgrounds would be photographic, while 30 percent would be 3D. Based on this, the original budget for the film was $16 million (when originally told the budget, Hollings misheard $60 million, and did a dramatic double take when he got the correct figure.) "At the time, the production flow would have involved scenes made up of background photos and images, with people plugged into that setting. Then, as the production developed, it became that we'd have to use more 3D, so the budget crept up to $22 million, and at the end, all-in, it was probably $45 million. I think we must have the lowest cost-per-shot effects for any contemporary movie. Because of the volume of the shots we completed, and the pipeline we introduced all under one roof, I think we managed 2,000 shots very economically. To help keep costs down, we used all off-the-shelf technology and did as little custom software development as possible."

IMAGES

01–03 Layered elements to build the *The Chronicle* interior.
04 Once motion blur, texture mapping, and lighting are applied to the image, *Sky Captain*'s finished look is a stylized hybrid of live action and animation.

[ SOURCE ]

[1] DARIN HOLLINGS, ORIGINAL INTERVIEW, MATT HANSON (10/2004)

[2] "RAIDERS OF THE LOST ART: THE ONE-MAN DESIGN BAND OF SKY CAPTAIN," JEFF BOND, *CFQ* (06/07/2004)

[3] SKY CAPTAIN SET VISIT, BRIAN CARROLL, COMINGSOON.NET (01/2004)

04

The movie was storyboarded, and then cut together using Final Cut Pro. Conran recorded a read-through with the actors in London, which he then took back to the *World of Tomorrow* production facility. It served as a temp track to pace the storyboards so they could work on these being substituted with Maya-built 3D animatics. The live action was all shot on three blue screen stages at London's Elstree Studios, using Sony's high-definition HDW-F900 camera.

Hollings worked on weekend schedule meetings with Director of Photography Eric Adkins, and production supervisor Matthew Feitshans to keep the shoot on track. They had a punishing schedule that required an average 37 shots a day for the 26 days of filming: "In terms of my responsibilities on set, on a high-definition monitor, I would compare the camera shot against an animatic of the scene using a simple switcher between the two images. When I was happy with the positioning, I'd call the DP, he'd consult with the Director, and we'd swap the stand-ins for the actors. I'd then go to the next stage where we were setting up the next shot.

"We basically did this round robin thing, moving from one set to the next, setting up in one, shooting in another, to keep the actors moving in and out of their trailers. Otherwise, that eats up time, and because we had a compressed shoot, five weeks for something that would normally be at least three times as long, we needed to use the time as efficiently as possible. It was so important we'd planned out the shots, and already given the animators ranges for the lenses and field of vision for settings when setting up the previsualizations. This meant everything was incredibly accurate, so we wasted as little time as possible setting up to shoot.

"Once we took all the scenes back to L.A., we had to redo a new set of animatics, to complement the digital cinematography of the shoot." With all the elements gathered, they were composited in black and white, to aid in matching all the different resolutions and image qualities together, the live-action, high-definition and photographic elements, and archive material. Once the final black and white was locked down, a small team then colorized the image. The subdued hues help cement an "otherness," of a future that never was, somewhere between the comic strip, newsreel archives of the 1930s, and hand-toned magazine illustrations from the period. A world of tomorrow that owes as much to microprocessors as it does to *Metropolis*.

2004
2003
2002
2001
2000
1999
1998
1997
1996
1995
1994
1993
1992
1991
1990
1989
1988
1987
1986
1985
1984
1983
1982

# 2046

**CREDITS**

DIRECTOR: WONG KAR-WAI

PRODUCTION DESIGNER: WILLIAM CHANG SUK PING

SCREENPLAY: WONG KAR-WAI

PRODUCERS: WONG KAR-WAI, YIMOU ZHANG

VISUAL EFFECTS: BUF COMPAGNIE

01

02

IMAGES

01  Wong Kar-Wai's *2046* is all about
reflections on the past, present, and
future, so there is judicious placement
of mirrored and reflective surfaces.
02  The deliberately dreamlike
rendering of a *2046* cityscape was
created using Buf's in-house
developed modeling, animation, paint,
and compositing toolset.

A romance set in the past, present, and future.
Time is refracted by Director Wong Kar-Wai into
an evocative love story, where dreamspace and
futurescape mesh and become indistinguishable.
Whereas other directors are using digital effects
to model monolithic structures and stage
outrageous space battles, Wong Kar-Wai
imagines how we dream the future to be—
ethereal, barely able to be grasped.

The shimmering crystalline landscape of
2046 Hong Kong was created by the Paris-based
effects shop, BUF Compagnie. "For Wong Kar-
Wai, using visual effects was a first and it was
our first Chinese movie. We went many times to
China to discover Chinese cities. During those
trips we took reference stills that we used to
create the City of 2046," states Guilliame Raffi,
VFX producer at Buf. The animation incorporates
recognizable Hong Kong landmarks, only now a
tubed trainline snakes between reflective
curtains of glass and steel skyscrapers that glow
pink, blue, yellow. The colors mirror the lush
cinematography of Wong Kar-Wei's long-time
collaborator, Christopher Doyle. When the film
segues into this future world, the train and other
interiors bring to mind *Barbarella* (1968). This is
sci-fi as imagined in the past—looking forward
has never been so nostalgic. A beguiling future
set in acid yellows, reds, and greens.

"Wong Kar-Wai works in a particular way, he
sends you on a track then reacts to your
interpretation of this track," states Visual Effects
Coordinator Guillaume Raffi. "That generates a
lot of material and concepts. In the end, a lot are
unused but that creates an interesting
development process."

In the film, nominally set in the 1960s, the
protagonist Chow Mo-Wan returns from
Singapore and finds a familiar room at a cheap
hotel in Wanchai, at the Oriental Hotel, room
2046. He starts writing a book, titled from the
room number. In the story, a train departs for
the year 2046 and those boarding it recover
their lost memories. Wong Kar-Wai's self-
referencing, the way his following films are
darker mirrors of the ones preceding—*Chungking
Express* (1994), and then *Fallen Angels* (1995), *In the
Mood for Love* (2000)—conjures up a fragmented
story between the remembered then and the
contemplated later. *2046* is a rare kind of science
fiction, perhaps the most alien kind: abstracted
and unearthly.

[ SOURCE ]

[1] GUILLIAME RAFFI, ORIGINAL
INTERVIEW, MATT HANSON (11/2004)

2004
2003
2002
2001
2000
1999
1998
1997
1996
1995
1994
1993
1992
1991
1990
1989
1988
1987
1986
1985
1984
1983
1982

**FILM**

**VISUAL EFFECTS**

+ **PRODUCTION I.G.**

# INNOCENCE: GHOST IN THE SHELL 2

Ø1

Ø2

**CREDITS**
DIRECTOR: **MAMORU OSHII**
PRODUCTION DESIGNER: **YOHEI TANEDA**
SHORT STORY: **MASAMUNE SHIROW**
SCREENPLAY: **MAMORU OSHII**
ART DIRECTOR: **SHUICHI HIRATA**
SPECIAL EFFECTS SUPERVISOR: **HIROYUKI HAYASHI**
PRODUCERS: **MITSUHISA ISHIKAWA, TOSHIO SUZUKI**

IMAGES

01 *Innocence* mixes 2D character animation with 3D models and painted backgrounds.
02 The opulent spires embody Oshii's vision of "Chinese Gothic."
03 Oshii's sensibilities transform past traditions into delirious future spectacles.

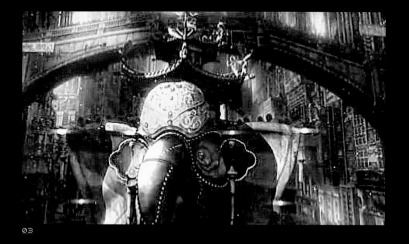

03

With *Innocence*, Mamoru Oshii pushes the envelope of what we know of as science fiction, and what we think of as animation. The acclaimed director of animation classics, *Patlabor* (1990, see page 38), and the original *Ghost in the Shell* (1995), as well as live-action films such as *Avalon* (2001), is a stylistic master akin to Ridley Scott, while having a philosophical bent similar to the Russian director, Andrei Tarkovsky. His works are meditations on what it means to be human as much as they are techno-actioners. His direction veers between Scott's intimate lens and Tarkovsky's remote gaze.

*Innocence: Ghost in the Shell 2* is set in 2032, when the line between humans and machines has been blurred almost beyond distinction. Humans have virtually forgotten what it means to be entirely human in both body and spirit, and the few humans that are left coexist with cyborgs—human spirits inhabiting entirely mechanized bodies—and dolls (robots with no human elements at all). *Innocence* continues the world created in Masumune Shirow's acclaimed original manga series, while adding stylistic flourishes and new possibilities.

We follow the adventures of Batou, a cyborg detective in the Government's covert anti-terrorist unit, Public Security Section 9. He is investigating the case of a gynoid—a pleasure robot created specifically for sexual companionship—who malfunctions and slaughters her owner. As Batou moves deeper into the mystery, he explores an anarchic zone outside of Tokyo, and travels through Oshii's conception of a "Chinese Gothic" world. Notably, this world is most astonishingly conveyed in the milieu of Locus Solus (meaning the "lonely place" in Latin).

"I have always watched and enjoyed European films since I was young," Oshii states. "I was always intrigued by the classic styles and old designs of the architecture and atmospheres of Eastern Europe because they are serene, beautiful, and nostalgic."[1] Visually, *Innocence* is directly influenced by classic films in the genre such as *Chinatown* (1974) by Roman Polanski and Robert Altman's screen adaptation of Raymond Chandler's novel, *The Long Goodbye* (1973). "The future I describe in the movies is actually not the future. It's the present, so if the future in the movies looks very dark and very sad, unfortunately, that's the way our present is."

>>>

"THE CITY OF ETOROFU BLENDS IMAGES OF THE NEW YORK CITY SKYLINE, A GOTHIC CATHEDRAL, AND HONG KONG'S DENSELY CLUSTERED HIGH-RISES... A CONSTRUCTION OF IMAGES DRAWN FROM THE MEMORY OF ITS CREATORS."
TARO IGARASHI

2004
2003
2002
2001
2000
1999
1998
1997
1996
1995
1994
1993
1992
1991
1990
1989
1988
1987
1986
1985
1984
1983
1982

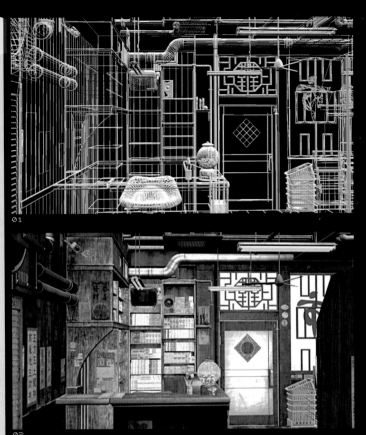

Ø1

Ø2

Ø3

Ø4

The topology of Oshii's futuristic fable is a delirious intermixture of retro and modern, introducing a geographically diverse range of architectural motifs; interiors that move between period Victoriana, and hi-tech labs. The exteriors are stunning—soon moving beyond the conventional fast-forwarded vision of a neon-illuminated dense inner-city squalor—fusing ideas of evolving Asian and historic medieval European architectural styles. Oshii sent concept photographer Haruhiko Higami to capture primary source material in Shanghai, Taipei, Germany, Italy, and New York. Production designer Yohei Taneda, art director Shuichi Hirata, and other production staff then filtered this imagery into the movie's exotic worldview.

The imagery reaches a zenith when Batou travels to the special economic zone of Etorofu, an unregulated hinterland north of Hokkaido, and a mist-covered cityscape of beautifully intertwining spires and turrets. It is here we spy the Locus Solus Company headquarters building, itself a Chinese mutation of Milan Cathedral. Taro Igarashi in his introduction to an exhibition of artwork from the film at Tokyo's Mori Urban Institute of the Future calls this "the city of the future as a construction of quotations.

The city of Etorofu thus blends images of the New York City skyline, a gothic cathedral, and Hong Kong's densely clustered high-rises. We might also call it a construction of images drawn from the memory of its creators. Higami has taken numerous photos of the Pudong district of Shanghai, a city which, driven by rapid economic growth, changed more in appearance during the 1990s than any other city in the world." [2]
>>>

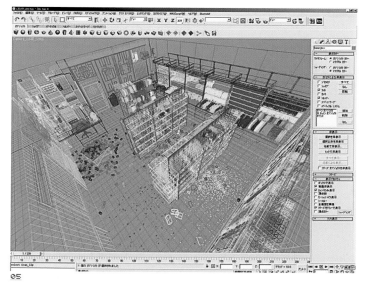

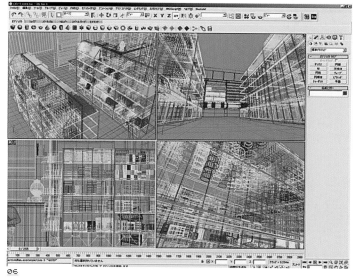

"I HAVE ALWAYS WATCHED AND ENJOYED
EUROPEAN FILMS. I WAS ALWAYS
INTRIGUED BY THE CLASSIC STYLES AND
OLD DESIGNS OF THE ARCHITECTURE AND
ATMOSPHERES OF EASTERN EUROPE
BECAUSE THEY ARE SERENE, BEAUTIFUL,
AND NOSTALGIC." MAMORU OSHII

IMAGES

01–04 Batou's local convenience
store, highly detailed and modeled in
Maya, is the setting for a surreally
tinged shoot-out. Screenshots
illustrate various stages of render,
from wireframe to final shot.
05–06 Screens from the animation
software Maya emphasize the intricate
modeling needed for the scene.
07 Finished still detailing the
aftermath and a wrecked store.

2004
2003
2002
2001
2000
1999
1998
1997
1996
1995
1994
1993
1992
1991
1990
1989
1988
1987
1986
1985
1984
1983
1982

01

02

Unlike the super-budgeted feature animations of Hollywood, Japanese animation has traditionally been developed on a much stricter budget. Thus 3D has only recently become commonly integrated into the industry's prestigious feature animation projects. An animation industry steeped in crafting hand-drawn 2D animation therefore, understandably, has decided not to throw away this tradition wholesale.

Kazuchika Kise, supervising key animator at Production I.G. (the company that also produced the sublime animé section of *Kill Bill: Vol.1* (2003)) makes this view clear: "I believe that there's no technology that comes close to what is created by the human hand. This is evident when one looks at famous art masterpieces. Because of the influence of manga in Japanese culture, it is hard to imagine that 2D culture will die out here. Japan may be unique in this sense, as we already have such as strong animation culture based around 2D." [3] So, animatics were produced from Oshii's ekonte (storyboards), and then elements of scenes were isolated to decide which were to be modeled using 3D packages, what of the background was to be painted. The characters were then hand drawn using a 2D style to add warmth and nuance to the animation.

*Innocence: Ghost in the Shell 2* was the first manga adaptation, and only the sixth animated film to be invited to compete at Cannes. A reward, perhaps, for creating a future environment that is so exquisitely crafted, it verges on fine art. "I'm interested in how far one can go with animation, and bringing my own personal reflections of life into it. I hope the subject will move the audience more as it is close to my own preoccupations. I want to push back the frontiers, and Innocence is a formulation of these ideas. It has gone beyond the limits and given shape to my ideas." [4]

[ SOURCES ]

[1] MAMORU OSHII INTERVIEW, WWW.NIDNIGHTEYE.COM, NICHOLAS RUCKA (23/09/2004)

[2] "ANIMÉ'S VISION OF THE ULTIMATE CITY OF THE FUTURE," INNOCENCE AND THE CITY EXHIBITION CATALOG, MUF (MORI URBAN INSTITUTE FOR THE FUTURE), TARO IGARASHI, TOKYO (01/2004)

[3] "A GLIMPSE INTO THE WORLD OF JAPANESE ANIMATION," JUSTIN LEACH, *CGNetworks* (10/2004)

[4] CANNES FILM FESTIVAL 2004 PRESS CONFERENCE

IMAGES

01 Oshii's "Chinese Gothic" style is best showcased in the film's most dreamlike and intoxicating chapter, when Batou's journey takes him to the remote reaches of Etorofu.
02 The parade passage of the feature is a transcendent evocation of religious and medieval pageantry—an audacious fit with the future timeline of *Innocence*.

# APPENDIX

**ANIMATICS:** crudely animated 3D storyboard to aid shot framing, sequencing and movement. Also see Previsualizations.

**ARCOLOGY:** a conflation of architecture and ecology. Based on Paolo Soleri's concept of 3D alternatives to urban sprawl, an arcology is usually seen in science fiction as a giant self-sufficient architectural structure.

**BANDE DESSINÉE:** French term for comic strips.

**BIOPUNK:** a subset of the cyberpunk genre, focussing on genetic manipulation and biotechnology rather than the hardwiring of humanity with electronic and digital machinery.

**BLUE SCREEN:** a pure blue screen used to create a clean matte, to define the areas of the image that are to be transparent. Once the subject is isolated as an element they can then be composited in a background. Alternately green screens can also be used, that offer better reviews when working with digital camera equipment.

**CEL-SHADING:** type of animation emulating the hand shading of cells in traditional animation, often to create an outlined cartoonish look.

**CG/CGI:** short for computer generated, and computer-generated imagery.

**COMPOSITE:** A final image made up of different and separately constructed layered elements.

**CYBERPUNK:** describes a dystopian future of grungy, hi-tech, virtual realities, and advanced technologies. A nihilistic combination of elements from film noir, detective novel, and Japanese animé in a science fiction setting.

**DEEP FUTURE:** science fiction in the far future timeline.

**DIGITAL BACKLOT:** term used to describe the breed of digital effects movie predominantly utilizing extensive green screen, digital effects, and virtual sets as part of the production.

**EKONTE:** Japanese term for storyboards.

**HARD SCIENCE FICTION:** a subgenre characterized by scientific accuracy and detail, often detailing astronomical or physical phenomena. Has increased its online presence with a recent upsurge in the "future documentary" brand of sci-fi film. Examples include *i, Robot*, and the *Patlabor* series.

**MACGUFFIN:** Coined by film director Alfred Hitchcock, the MacGuffin is a plot device to describe an object of vital importance to characters in a story, but which may be irrelevant to the narrative.

**MOCAP:** short for motion capture, a method of capturing fluid human movement, turning it into digital information to use in animation and CG work.

**POST-CYBERPUNK:** emphasizes the social aspects of Earthbound technology, rejecting spacebound adventure and alien technology. The post-cyberpunk genre benefits from being written after the full effects of the information revolution and ubiquitous internet use.

**PREVIS (SOMETIMES PREVIZ):** short for previsualization. Animated storyboards, and initial renders of effects shots are essential in planning how a scene is to be composited and fully realized.

**RENDER:** a depiction of a digital effect must be rendered using appropriate animation or imaging software. Renders can be complete, or in various stages of process. Early renders, for example, may be comprised of fewer polygons, and detailing such as texture maps and lighting.

**SF:** short for science fiction or speculative fiction, to more readily take in science fiction and fantasy genres.

**SCIENCE FICTION:** fiction that principally deals with imagined or extrapolated science and technology in a story setting most commonly in the future.

**SCIENCE FANTASY:** fiction that builds more fantastical futures and alternate realities, often detailing alien species and environments, or "lost" technology. The *Star Wars* series is the prime example of this genre.

**SOFT SCIENCE FICTION:** This sub-genre is more interested in exploring themes regarding human philosophy, sociology, politics, and psychology. Technology and science are deemphasized, unless they impact on the primary themes. Frank Herbert's *Dune* is widely seen to have popularized this type of sci-fi.

**SPACE OPERA:** action-oriented space adventures. Takes in the pulp sci-fi of *Star Wars* as well as the more scientifically grounded *Starship Troopers*. *Star Trek* lies somewhere in the middle of this range.

**SPECIAL EFFECTS:** on-set pyrotechnics and physical effects.

**STEAMPUNK:** unlike the cyberpunk focus on nanotechnology, and digitally augmented reality, including body implants, steampunk focuses on an environment filled with Victorian-era hi-tech, Lovecraftian, and medieval elements.

**STORYBOARDS:** frame-by-frame shot sequence illustration.

**TECH NOUVEAU:** also called zoomorphism or neo-organicism. Architecture and design taking overt cues from natural structures and organisms.

**VISUAL EFFECTS:** covers both optical or CG effects within a film.

## SOFTWARE

**3DS MAX:** 3D Studio Max is a highly customizable, scaleable 3D animation, modeling and rendering solution.
www.discreet.com

**AFTER EFFECTS:** Adobe's pioneering video compositing software.
www.adobe.com

**COMBUSTION:** Discreet's comprehensive desktop motion graphics, compositing solution.
www.discreet.com

**LIGHTWAVE 3D:** 3D animation production pipeline, comprising modeling tools, character animation.
www.newtek.com

**MASSIVE:** developed in conjunction with WETA for *The Lord of the Rings: The Return of the King,* Massive is the premier 3D animation system for generating crowd-related visual effects.
www.massivesoftware.com

**MAYA:** integrated 3D modeling, animation, effects, and rendering solution.
www.alias.com

**MENTAL RAY:** Rendering solution by Alias, streamlines the output of photorealistic to stylized visualizations.
www.alias.com

**PHOTOSHOP:** Adobe's groundbreaking still image manipulation software.
www.adobe.com

**RENDERMAN:** Rendering solution for CG imagery, using advanced shading, ray tracing, and motion blur anti-aliasing.
www.pixar.com/renderman

# SELECTED BIBLIOGRAPHY / VIEWING / READING

**SELECTED SCIENCE FICTION FILM**

2001: A Space Odyssey, Stanley Kubrick (1968)
2010: Odyssey 2, Peter Hyams (1984)
2046, Wong Kar-Wai (2004)
A.I.: Artificial Intelligence, Steven Spielberg (2001)
Akira, Katsuhiro Otomo (1988)
Alien, Ridley Scott (1979)
Aliens, James Cameron (1986)
Alien³, David Fincher (1992)
Alien: Resurrection, Jean-Pierre Jeunet (1997)
Alphaville, Jean-Luc Godard (1965)
Animatrix, The, Various (2003)
Appleseed, Shinji Aramaki (2004)
Avalon, Mamoru Oshii (2001)
Barbarella, Roger Vadim (1968)
Batman, Tim Burton (1989)
Blade Runner, Ridley Scott (1982)
Brazil, Terry Gilliam (1985)
Casshern, Kazuaki Kiriya (2004)
City of Lost Children, The, Jeunet & Caro (1995)
Clockwork Orange, A, Stanley Kubrick (1971)
Close Encounters of the Third Kind, Steven Spielberg (1977)
Code 46, Michael Winterbottom (2003)
CQ, Roman Coppola (2001)
Cube, Vincenzo Natali (1997)
Dark City, Alex Proyas (1998)
Dernier Combat, Le, Luc Besson (1983)
Dune, David Lynch (1984)
Dr. Strangelove or How I Learned to Stop Worrying
and Love the Bomb, Stanley Kubrick (1964)
Equilibrium, Kurt Wimmer (2002)
Event Horizon, Paul WS Anderson (1997)
eXistenZ, David Cronenberg (1999)
Fifth Element, The, Luc Besson (1997)
Final Fantasy: The Spirits Within, Hironobu Sakaguchi
& Moto Sakakibara (2001)
Gattaca, Andrew Niccol (1997)
Ghost in the Shell, Mamoru Oshii (1995)
Immortel, Enki Bilal (2004)
Innocence: Ghost in the Shell 2, Mamoru Oshii (2004)
i, Robot, Alex Proyas (2004)
Judge Dredd, Danny Cannon (1995)
Johnny Mnemonic, Robert Longo (1995)
La Jetée, Chris Marker (1962)
Logan's Run, Michael Anderson (1976)
Matrix, The, Andy & Larry Wachowski (1999)
Matrix Reloaded, The, Andy & Larry Wachowski (2003)
Matrix Revolutions, The, Andy & Larry Wachowski (2003)
Memories, Koji Morimoto, Tensai Okamuro,
& Katsuhiro Ôtomo (1996)
Metropolis, Fritz Lang (1927)
Metropolis, Rintaro (2001)
Minority Report, Steven Spielberg (2002)
Natural City, Byung-Chin Min (2003)
Patlabor, Mamoru Oshii (1990)
Patlabor WXIII, Takuji Endo, Fumihiko Takayama (2002)
Planet of the Apes, Franklin J. Schaffner (1968)
Red Spectacles, Mamoru Oshii (1987)
Robocop, Paul Verhoeven (1987)
Sky Captain and the World of Tomorrow, Kerry Conran (2004)
Solaris, Andrei Tarkovsky (1972)
Solaris, Steven Soderbergh (2002)

Star Trek: The Motion Picture, Robert Wise (1979)
Star Wars Episode I: The Phantom Menace, George Lucas (1999)
Star Wars Episode II: Attack of the Clones, George Lucas (2002)
Star Wars Episode III: Revenge of the Sith, George Lucas (2005)
Star Wars Episode IV: A New Hope, George Lucas (1977)
Star Wars Episode V: The Empire Strikes Back, George Lucas (1980)
Star Wars Episode VI: Return of the Jedi, George Lucas (1983)
Strange Days, Kathryn Bigelow (1995)
Swallowtail Butterfly, Shunji Iwai (1996)
Terminator, The, James Cameron (1984)
Terminator 2: Judgement Day, James Cameron (1991)
Tetsuo, Shinya Tsukamoto (1988)
Tetsuo II: Body Hammer, Shinya Tsukamoto (1992)
Things to Come, William Cameron Menzies (1936)
THX 1138, George Lucas (1971)
Total Recall, Paul Verhoeven (1990)
Tron, Steven Lisberger (1982)
Tycho Moon, Enki Bilal (1996)
Twelve Monkeys, Terry Gilliam (1995)
Until the End of the World, Wim Wenders (1991)
Wonderful Days, Kim Mun-Saeng (2003)


**BOOKS & PUBLICATIONS**

Alien Zone: Cultural theory and Contemporary Science Fiction Cinema,
Ed. Annette Kuhn (Verso, 1990)
Alien Zone 2: The Spaces of Science Fiction Cinema,
Ed. Annette Kuhn (Verso, 2000)
Architecture & Animation,
Ed. Bob Fear, Architectural Design Series (2000)
Architecture & Film: Vol 2
Ed. Bob Fear, Architectural Design Series (2001)
Cultvision: Idn Special 02 (Gingko Press,2003)
Film Architecture: Set Designs from 'Metropolis' to 'Blade Runner',
Dietrich Neumann (Prestel Publishing Ltd, 2000)
Future Noir: The Making of Blade Runner, Paul Sammon (Orion, 1997)
Gilliam on Gilliam, Ed. Ian Christie (Faber & Faber,1999)
Production Design & Art Direction (Screencraft),
Peter Ettedgui (Rotovision, 1999)
Metropolis of Tomorrow, The, H. Ferriss (Architectural Press, 1986)
Science Fiction Film, J.P. Telotte (Cambridge University Press, 2001)
Sci-fi Architecture,
Ed. Maggie Toy,  Architectural Design Series (1999)

**MAGAZINES**

Cinefex
Cinescape
SFX
Wired

**WEBSITES**

Animation flash (www.anm.com)
CGNetworks (www.cgnetworks.com)
Cinescape (www2.cinescape.com)
Computer Graphics World (www.cgw.com)
Millimeter (www.millimeter.com)
VFXPro.com (www.vfxpro.com)
VFXWorld (www.vfxworld.com)

**FURTHER RESOURCES**

www.visint.tv/scifi

# PICTURE CREDITS

COURTESY AND/OR COPYRIGHT OF:

*2001: A Space Odyssey*, MGM/The Kobal Collection
*2046*, Jet Tone Films/Océan Films
*A.I*, Amblin Entertainment, Dreamworks/Warner Brothers
*Alien*, 20th Century Fox/The Kobal Collection
*Aliens*, 20th Century Fox/The Kobal Collection
*Alien3*, 20th Century Fox/The Kobal Collection
*Alien: Resurrection*, 20th Century Fox/The Kobal Collection
*Appleseed*, Geneon Entertainment
*Batman*, Warner Bros/The Kobal Collection, NYC photo by Andreas Feininger/Time & Life Pictures
*Blade Runner*, Ladd Company/Warner Bros/The Kobal Collection
*Brazil*, 20th Century Fox
*Casshern*, Shochiku, Dreamworks
*City of Lost Children, The* Lumiere/Entertainment in Video
*Code 46*, Revolution/Verve Pictures
*Dark City*, New Line/The Kobal Collection
*Dune*, Universal/The Kobal Collection, Ron Miller
*Fifth Element, The*, Columbia/Tri-Star/The Kobal Collection
*Johnny Mnemonic*, Limited Partnership/Alliance/The Kobal Collection, Braid
*Immortel*, Duran
*Innocence: Ghost in the Shell 2*, Production IG, Dreamworks Pictures
*Matrix Reloaded, The*, Warner Bros, Tippett Studios
*Memories*, Memories Production Committee
*Metropolis*, Tezuka Productions/Metropolis Project
*Metropolis*, UFA/The Kobal Collection
*Minority Report*, Amblin Entertainment, 20th Century Fox/Dreamworks Pictures, Alex McDowell
*i, Robot*, 20th Century Fox, Stephan Martiniere, Milwaukee Art Museum photo by Alan Karchmer/Esto, Asimo by Honda
*Natural City*, Optimum Releasing
*Patlabor*, Manga Entertainment
*Sky Captain and the World of Tomorrow*, Paramount, World of Tomorrow, Darin Hollings
*Solaris* (Tarkovsky), Mosfilm/The Kobal Collection
*Solaris* [Soderbergh], Lightstorm Entertainment/20th Century Fox/The Kobal Collection, Bob Marshak. Tim Flattery
*Starship Troopers*, Tri-Star/Touchstone Pictures
*Star Wars*, Lucasfilm/20th Century Fox/The Kobal Collection
*Star Wars: The Empire Strikes Back*, Lucasfilm/20th Century Fox/The Kobal Collection
*Star Wars: The Phantom Menace*, Lucasfilm/20th Century Fox/The Kobal Collection
*Star Wars: Attack of the Clones*, Lucasfilm/20th Century Fox/The Kobal Collection
*THX 1138*, American Zoetrope/Warner Bros/The Kobal Collection
*Total Recall*, Carolco/Tri-Star/The Kobal Collection
*Tron*, Walt Disney Pictures//The Kobal Collection
*Wonderful Days*, Tinhouse Korea

# INDEX

# INDEX

# ACKNOWLEDGMENTS

DEDICATED TO J.M.H., WHO ALWAYS
THOUGHT I WAS ON ANOTHER PLANET.

TO LEONIE, FOR THE ORIGINAL CONCEPT,
GUIDANCE, EDITING, INFINITE PATIENCE
AND EMOTIONAL SUPPORT. HARPER AND
PASHA FOR THE INSPIRATION. PAUL
FARRINGTON FOR HIS BRILLIANT DESIGN,
ELECTRONIC MUSIC, AND ABSURD
MUSINGS. THANKS TO ALL AT ROTOVISION
FOR GIVING ME THE OPPORTUNITY TO WRITE
ANOTHER BOOK WITH THEM.

I AM ESPECIALLY GRATEFUL TO ALL THOSE
WHO AGREED TO BE INTERVIEWED FOR THIS
PUBLICATION, AND EVERYONE WHO HELPED
MAKE IT HAPPEN IN SOME WAY, INCLUDING:

AKIRA, PRODUCTION IG
MOLLY BRUNS, JACOB & KOLE
KUN CHANG
BERGE GARABEDIAN (JOBLO)
HEATHER, SKOURAS AGENCY
CRAIG HAYES, JIM BLOOM, TIPPETT STUDIOS
DARIN HOLLINGS
KAY HWANG, TINHOUSE
ALLISON KLEIN, PATRICK TATOPOULOS,
PATRICK TATOPOULOS DESIGNS, INC.
MARVIN LEVY, KRISTIN STARK,
DREAMWORKS
PATTY MACK
ALEX MCDOWELL
STEPHAN MARTINIERE
RON MILLER
OLIVIER MOUROUX, DREAMWORKS
OWEN PATERSON
JACQUEMIN PIEL, DURAN
DIANA PRIVITERA, OPTIMUM RELEASING
GUILLUAME RAFFI, BUF COMPAGNIE
PAUL M. SAMMON
WILLIAM SANDELL
ERIC SWENSON
J. MIRA YONG, THE GERSH AGENCY
AND ALL THE PRODUCTION COMPANIES,
STUDIOS, & DISTRIBUTORS INVOLVED.

MY CURRENT TOP 15 SF FILMS:
*2001: A Space Odyssey*
*Blade Runner*
*Avalon*
*Solaris* (1972 original)
*Alien* quadrilogy
*Strange Days*
*Akira*
*Gattaca*
*Matrix* trilogy
*Star Wars* trilogy (IV-VI)
*Minority Report*
*Casshern*
*Dune*
*Twelve Monkeys*
*Tron*